Market your

business

Australia • Canada • Mexico • Singapore • Spain • United Kingdom • United States

THOMSON
✶ ™
LEARNING

Market Your Business- A guide for small hospitality businesses

Copyright © Hospitality Training Foundation and Thomson Learning 2000

The Thomson Learning logo is a registered trademark used herein under licence.

For more information, contact Thomson Learning, Berkshire House, 168–173 High Holborn, London, WC1V 7AA or visit us on the World Wide Web at: http://www.thomsonlearning.co.uk

British Library Cataloguing-in-Publication Data
A catalogue record for this book is available from the British Library

ISBN 1-86152-718-7

First published 2000 by Macmillan Press Ltd
Reprinted 2000 by Thomson Learning

Design, typesetting and graphics by Lloyds Publishing & Training, Llanidloes, Powys

Illustrations by Dave Bell, Carshalton Beeches, Surrey

Printed by Antony Rowe

Acknowledgements

The publishers and authors would like to express sincere thanks to the following for their help in reviewing the text:

Rose Alderman, Milton Keynes College

Hugh Becker, The Norman Richardson House Trust, Darlington

Adrian Clark, The Tourism Society, London

Andrew Cole, Pratt's Hotel, Bath

Julian Demetriadi, Apostrophe, London

Lucia Gillett, The Rangeworthy Court Hotel, Bristol

David Kingsbury, Premier Training, Middlesex

Peter Russum, E Russum & Sons Ltd, Rotherham

and special thanks to

Caterer & Hotelkeeper, The Restaurant Business and *Hotel & Restaurant Magazine* for permission to draw on published articles (as acknowledged in the text).

The Hospitality Training Foundation (HtF) is the National Training Organisation for the hospitality industry. HtF represents hospitality employers on all issues relating to education and training.

Part of HtF's work is the Quality Business initiative, a three-year programme to provide relevant support for small hospitality businesses.

The Quality Business initiative is funded by the Department for Education and Employment (DfEE) and also includes CD-Roms, audio tapes, leaflets and posters.

Market your
business

Contents

Foreword

Running a small hospitality business, you have limited resources and great demands on your time. You know that luck and intuition are not sufficient to grow your business in today's competitive marketplace. Nevertheless, you do have strong advantages. In particular, the personal stamp that you put on the business, and which gives an edge to your hospitality that customers really value.

This guide helps you to take stock of your business, build on its special appeal, and communicate that appeal to a wider, and, crucially, a receptive audience through careful targeting. Read it from cover to cover – this will not take long – or dip into sections or pages, as needs and interests dictate. The guide will:

- give you an appreciation of the many different ways you can bring in more customers to your business, encourage them to spend more, and develop a strong, loyal clientele

- encourage a balance of activities, so that you do not rely too much on reputation, for example, and are quick to notice a change in your customer make-up

- help you plan your marketing, increase the success rate, get the best value from your marketing spend, and learn from what you do

- stimulate ideas through the case studies and expert opinion, gleaned from the industry's principal journals.

You will find people enthusiastic about different marketing methods, while others have a low opinion. Behind this divergence of views is the mixed experience and skills in applying the particular method – good and poor techniques from which you can learn. Or it could be the product and services being promoted – ultimately, the success of marketing depends on the consistently high quality of what you are providing, as judged by your customers.

1 Take stock of your business

Would you like to attract more customers or guests? Would you like them to spend more? Would you like to offer the products and services which satisfy the customers of today and the future? Marketing can help you do this, and there is a wide choice – advertising, direct mail, public relations, promotional offers, a website are just some ways. In order to obtain effective results, real value for your investment, begin by taking a step back. Get an objective view, to add to and shape what you already know of your business and its customers into a well-constructed marketing analysis. From this, you can develop a clear, affordable and practical plan to grow your business.

Who are your customers?

What are the main characteristics about the people whom your business attracts at the moment? Search for the common elements. Where they come from and what they are doing may be quickly apparent: local people, tourists, business people, students, walkers and so forth.

Within such groupings, there are sub-categories that tell you a little more. Age, sex, income, job or profession, where they live, size of group (on their own, with others, with a family), method of travel, distance travelled, are the principal ones.

To get a clear understanding of his business, this publican has ranked the main market for each session

	Mon-Thur lunch	Mon-Thur eve	Friday lunch	Friday eve	lunch	eve	Sunday lunch	eve
Office workers	1		1					
Pensioners	5		2		3			1
Professionals	2							
Shoppers	3		3					
Tourists	3	2	4		2		2	
Young people		1		1		1		
Family groups					1		1	

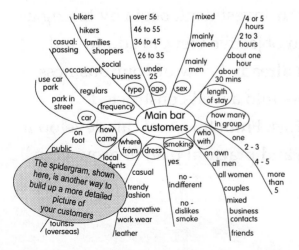

The spidergram, shown here, is another way to build up a more detailed picture of your customers

When a hunch is not enough

First the run-down pub would be turned into an informal style Avins Bridge Restaurant and Bar. Then the profits would be used to refurbish the four bedrooms to offer bed and breakfast.

When the restaurant fell short of its projected income for several months, Chris and Becky Barnard went to their bank for the development money. With no marketing plan to show, nor clear ideas on how to build their market, the answer was 'no'.

Turning to the local Business Link for help, the Barnards were advised to focus on who their customers were, and why they chose Avins Bridge. Becky was soon able to get useful answers: customers were typically in the 40–50 age bracket, a high percentage were company owners and directors, the restaurant's ambience and style of food were strong draws.

12.2.98

Caterer & Hotelkeeper

Keeping local trade at a cost

Changing the public areas would upset the locals, some of whom come in twice a day and view the Royal Oak in Exmoor National Park as an extension of their homes. Kevan Draper has had to accept that this means a lower grading by the tourist board, because of the weighting given to public areas. Room prices, which reflect the much improved bedrooms, also seem expensive for the number of stars.

Fortunately, around 50% of trade is from repeat business, and some 60% of new business comes from Camra's *Good Beer Guide*.

18.9.97

Caterer & Hotelkeeper, Jenny Webster

Why are they your customers?

There are two dimensions to this stage of your analysis:

- *the purpose of their visit*: to eat, drink or sleep; to relax, take exercise, or be entertained; to do business with local companies, be with their family, or see historical buildings, for example

- *what draws them to your establishment rather than one of your competitors*: location, prices, external appearance of building, good reputation, recommendation, through the tourist board, advertisement, guide entry.

Often the categories are a mix of these: the precise words are less important than the process of analysis. Choose groups which best describe your business's customers. The aim of going through this process is to inform your marketing activities:

- who you should target

- what your message should be

- how you might reach these people with your message.

It is an evolving, on-going process with no absolute rights or wrongs.

Remote location, strong appeal

There is no pool of customers in a remote location. Nevertheless owners of the Old Pines restaurant with rooms in Spean Bridge, Inverness-shire tripled their gross income within eight years of taking over the business. About two-thirds of custom is repeat or recommended. Most are tourists, some come every year. Sukie and Bill Barber also rely on free guides to spread the word, paying for only 11% of the publicity they receive.

'Besides being off the beaten track, the Barbers have imposed a smoking ban and got rid of their drinks licence, putting the onus on diners to remember to bring a bottle. So what are they doing to win this all-important repeat trade?' Rosalind Mullen asks:

- **offering value for money** – prices are carefully pitched between B&B and hotel rates, and include tea on arrival, soft drinks and even laundry

- **welcome for families** – guests' children often join Bill and Sukie's own offspring for supper in the kitchen, then gravitate to the play room, while the parents enjoy a break

- **sociable atmosphere** – observing who gets on with whom in the lounge, Bill works out the seating plan at the one large dinner table

- **very high standard of cooking** – Sukie appreciates that food is the backbone of the business and continually strives to improve it, adding new dimensions to favourite dishes.

In the winter room occupancy drops to 12% or below, and much of this is weekenders from Glasgow, Edinburgh and Dundee. To supplement revenue, Sukie runs training courses for the local enterprise company and does cookery demonstrations.

2.7.98

Caterer & Hotelkeeper, Rosalind Mullen

When visually impaired guests find a hotel where they feel comfortable, it appears to draw them back like a magnet. They come with sighted friends and family, recommend it to others with sight difficulties and provide a high level of repeat business.

Andy Moran, general manager of Belmont Hotel, Llandudno, speaking to Bob Gledhill, *Caterer & Hotelkeeper*

What affects your business?

As you think about your customers, you are likely to make observations such as the favourable impact of reviews in this year's guides to eating out and where to stay, how the repainted exterior and new signage are attracting passing-by trade. Tourist and leisure facilities in the locality, or a new road, may be drawing greater numbers of visitors.

There may be the challenging developments, such as a new bar or restaurant which has won popularity thanks to trendy decor and youthful staff. Or parking restrictions in your street.

And then there are those hopefully rare events, such as flash floods and oil spills, which bring practical problems and the publicity that puts off tourists, holiday-makers and leisure visitors.

... and how has it developed?

Look back on changes while you have been running your business, such as:

- what you offer customers: prices, products, level of comfort, range of services and facilities

- your customers' requirements: stay for shorter time, want entertainment, eat less meat, fewer smoke, more come from mainland Europe

- activities of similar businesses: how they have affected your trade, their successes and failures

- other changes affecting customer behaviour: increasing popularity of short breaks, more older people, more single parents, decline in manufacturing industry.

Learning the hard way

Their first June was a disappointment for Katherine and Simon Hodgson, owners of the Yarcombe Inn. Many regulars stayed at home to watch the Euro football championships, and the farmers were 'working very long hours ... and don't have time to eat or pop in for a drink after work – we've noticed a dramatic drop in custom. But at least we know and will be able to budget for next year.'

But the quiet month gave the Hodgsons plenty of time to plan promotional activities, including:

- advertising in press and tourist guides in the Midlands (an important source of visitors to Devon)

- a programme of theme nights to bring in locals, including a pig roast night, medieval banquet, and the Rocky Horror Show party for halloween

- advertising in the motorbike press, to attract foreign bikers (the inn is on one of the routes from a south coast ferry port).

25.7.96

Caterer & Hotelkeeper, Rachel Mackett

After a Michael Winner attack

A scathing review by Michael Winner in *The Sunday Times* hit trade at Henllys Hall in Beaumaris, Anglesey and demoralised staff. But general manager Nick Day was determined to draw something positive from the nightmare. He got staff to agree in which areas Winner had made valid points, and used these to improve procedures and raise the level of service. It was encouraging too, to see many letters of support from loyal customers appear in the local press.

8.10.98

Caterer & Hotelkeeper, Jenny Webster

What is special about your business?

Focus on your strong points: those which clearly appeal to customers, those which bring regulars back and lead to recommendations and favourable reviews, those which distinguish your business from competitors.

It is essential to talk to customers and ask their views directly. For some businesses, a short questionnaire or comment card helps this process. It can be placed with the bill at the end of the meal or stay, left on restaurant or bar tables, or in guest rooms. Replies can be anonymous, or space left for the customer's name and address, to claim the prize draw each month (a way to encourage responses) or to be added to the mailing list for details of special offers.

Staff can play a valuable role in providing feedback, passing on comments customers make to them, and asking customers for their views – they are likely to need your help to decide the most effective way of doing this.

Customers contribute views

With the help of consultants Triton (appointed through *Caterer & Hotelkeeper's* Lifesaver project), Richard and Helen Davies focused on existing customers by:

- inviting eight regulars to a buffet meal and drinks, during which a Triton researcher (who had the advantage of being independent) presented them with varying menus at different prices, and some design ideas
- asking a random selection of customers to complete a brief questionnaire, with a special prize draw as an incentive to participate.

Strong points identified included:

- goodwill which the business had developed
- the Davies's honest and dedicated approach to food quality (however only five out of ten customers said the food was excellent)
- decor in the old part of the building was attractive
- despite unfavourable comments about the (new) restaurant decor, it portrayed a clean image
- the couple worked very hard, and fully appreciated the importance of improving quality and were quick to learn and willing to take on new ideas.

15.10.92

Caterer & Hotelkeeper, Catey Hillier

Staff involved in changes

The only pub in Mosterton, a small village on the main tourist route into the West country, the Admiral was not taking full advantage of its location. As a result of standing back to analyse their business, David and Esme Mitchell decided to take the food operation upmarket.

At the same time, the Mitchells worked hard to get their staff involved in the business success. As an incentive, visits to a competiting pub which led to three ideas for improving profits, were paid for. One change is that the specials black board is now carried to the customers' table by the waiter or waitress. Sales of starters and puddings have increased by 30%.

In six months some 3% has been added to the overall gross profit of the Admiral.

26.11.98

Caterer & Hotelkeeper

What are your plans for the business?

Do you have ambitions to expand, to open other branches? Is there interest on a loan to pay, and the loan itself to repay? Or are you more modestly looking for a better return on the business as it stands now, and to generate the funds to continue to improve the facilities you provide customers?

What are the implications of winning more business? Will you have to take on more staff and invest in more equipment? If you do have to employ more staff, what happens during the quieter business periods?

The problem of staffing and skill levels should be thought through before the opening, a new menu, or any major change in policy. One chef proprietor changed his menu to include some superb dishes but didn't take into account the time and cost needed to prepare each dish. The food was outstanding but everyone got fed up waiting. He had to redesign the menu.

Melvyn Greene, *Caterer & Hotelkeeper*

Keeping up with the market

The formality of the dining room at Calcot Manor, Gloucestershire was felt by Richard Ball, managing director, to be out of step with what today's customer wanted, and did not suit the farm house feel of the building generally.

A conservatory was added, the decor, table and seating changed, a more relaxed style of service introduced, and prices lowered. An extra 30 covers could now be catered for in the new Brasserie, taking the total to 70.

At the same time, a loyalty scheme was introduced. A small fee, paid yearly, entitles participants – already 150 have signed up – to 10% off their bill each time they dine at the Manor. Many more local residents now eat at the Manor: up from 15% to 40%.

When market trends next demand it, Richard is ready to alter his business again.

29.10.98

Caterer & Hotelkeeper

Turning the corner after 26 years

After 26 years, Malcolm Sissons decided it was time to inject new life into The Lodge Grill, in Bromley's shopping mall. He spoke to customers and conducted a written survey.

Sisson's daughter, Nicola, spearheaded a new delivery service taking burgers, baguettes, salads and sandwiches to local addresses, an outside eating area in front of the restaurant during the summer, and the opening of a brasserie on the first floor on Friday and Saturday evenings. Sissons Catering Services has been built up through direct visits to local schools and businesses. Table tent cards, supplier-assisted promotions, and advertisements in the local press have also increased trade at The Lodge. New menus and uniforms complete the change.

'Now,' says Sissons, 'We serve the products they want, with the service they seek, in the surroundings they desire.'

All staff are encouraged to share their ideas about the operation at monthly meetings.

23.1.97

Janet Harmer reporting on the winners of the 1997 *Caterer & Hotelkeeper's* Peacock Awards

2 Identify opportunities

You have stood back and reflected on where your business is today. Now is the time to get ideas together for reaching new customers, and encouraging existing customers to spend more. Don't exclude anything for the moment. Be willing to explore every avenue. Later you can focus on which ideas have potential, are likely to work best, and how you can get them underway.

Build on strengths

When you set out to market your business it makes sense to begin with those aspects that are already popular or well thought of by customers. If you can reach other people with similar requirements, then you stand to expand business significantly.

What are you good at? What have been your successes? What do your customers really like? Think about the products, facilities and services, the skills, experience and attitude to customers of your employees, the location and surroundings, how customers get to you and how long their journey takes.

Be disciplined in your analysis. It's customers' views that matter. You may deservedly be proud of the new kitchen, but the food is what customers judge.

Have another look at the information you collected in conversations and questionnaires from customers. There may be aspects of your business which customers value, yet you have not realised their significance. For instance, a high standard of cleanliness consistently heads the list of requirements in surveys by tourist boards and consumer organisations of what customers look for in hospitality establishments.

Accept disappointments. If the wine list which is your pride and joy does not get highly rated, consider how to rationalise it. Perhaps the customers you thought would be attracted by such a list are not getting the message, or there are other places which appeal to them more, or you have over-estimated the interest in unusual wines in your locality.

Friendly welcome beats weather

In January, with severe flooding in the area, Claire Mitchem, owner of the Whittles farm in Hatch Beauchamp, thought it best to advise the BBC filming crew to stay elsewhere. Despite the weather and being able to afford more expensive accommodation, the crew opted to make the trek to Whittles farm. Claire puts this down to her friendly style of hospitality. Each Christmas, she receives greetings from former guests as far away as Australia.

Hotel & Catering Business

Payback from guest profiles

To build up a picture of the 'standard' guest takes time. For Beppo Buchanan-Smith, director of Isle of Eriska, a privately owned 17 bedroom hotel on the west coast of Scotland, the effort is well worthwhile: 'It means we can satisfy and exceed the expectations of our customers.'

Nevertheless, July and August present a particular challenge with a wider cross section of customers than at other times of the year. 'Instead of altering our product too drastically for each market, we stretch it to meet as many needs as possible. Quality and value are the unifying thread.'

10.9.98

Caterer & Hotelkeeper, Reader Diaries

Word power

By chatting to customers Keith Read has got to know about their lifestyles, and such details as their average age, how often and where they go on holiday. From this and through regular mailshots and newsletters selected from a large database, he soon transformed the run-down Leathern Bottel he bought in the early 1990s to a successful restaurant.

10.9.98

Caterer & Hotelkeeper, David Tarpey

Identify the weaknesses

Every business has some weaknesses. In a small operation, this may be that you cannot always be by the phone. Acknowledging weaknesses helps you plan corrective action: perhaps installing more telephone extensions and using an answering service.

Other weaknesses you may have to live with, but at least you can lessen their impact, for example, warning that children should be accompanied by adults while playing in your large gardens, because of the unprotected ponds. A restaurant without a licence can invite customers to bring their own wines, turning a potential weakness into an attraction.

Keep the focus on what customers perceive as weaknesses. Restricted storage space in a pub cellar is not a weakness when the customers appreciate a choice of quality beers. Small bedrooms are not a weakness if your tariff offers value-for-money to low budget customers.

Weaknesses identified

Consultants Triton (appointed through *Caterer & Hotelkeeper's* Lifesaver project) also helped Richard and Helen Davies identify the weaknesses of their business (see page 5):

- while in a pleasant rural location, the distance to travel was significant, particularly for business users
- poor external signposting, main entrance not immediately identifiable, unattractive external appearance of building
- restaurant extension gave no feeling of comfort
- the pictures in the restaurant, loaned from a local gallery and available to buy, were too varied in style, and customers feared they would be subjected to a sales pitch during their meal
- no host front-of-house or visible supervision
- poor service
- weak financial control, poor customer skills and staff management
- little marketing or promotional activity.

15.10.92

Caterer & Hotelkeeper, Catey Hillier

New image

Trying to change the locals' perception of the Yarcombe Inn, near Honiton in Devon, was one of the biggest problems for new owners Simon and Katherine Hodgson. 'The inn had a bad reputation. We are working hard to promote its new aspects and the family feel of the pub.'

A full-time bar attendant and five part-time staff have been employed to help the Hodgsons create a family-orientated pub. Food is another key change. Simon is keen to push the new lunchtime menu to local businesses.

27.6.96

Caterer & Hotelkeeper, Rachel Mackett

Customers will judge your business on the skills and attitudes of your staff: you are not always given a second chance to rectify their shortcomings. Strive to recruit the best and build them into a team that reflects your management style and aspirations.

Michael Sargent in *Caterer & Hotelkeeper*

Learn from your competitors

In good times, it is easy to shut your mind to what competitors are doing. This is a risky approach. Once your previously loyal customers do try and find they prefer a competitor, it is very difficult to woo them back.

Begin by looking at similar businesses to yours. Observe what is in the public domain and listen to what customers, locals, your staff and friends are saying. What prices do they charge? What facilities, services and products do they offer, and what improvements and changes have they made? What marketing are they doing?

Then look at your competitors at a more general level. If local shopkeepers, some in direct competition, have collaborated to win back business from out-of-town complexes through a loyalty card scheme, a similar tactic may help you. When a specialist shop or attraction lures customers from far afield, how can you share its appeal?

New competitors are likely to bring a fresh approach to tackling your market. Be ready to learn from their successes – special offers to bring in customers who become regulars thanks to the quality service. And their disappointments – high drink prices mean they only attract the curious who try anywhere once.

A new focus on wine by the glass increased business for Ian Vipond, chef-patron of the New Inn, a pub on the edge of the Yorkshire Dales. To maintain customers' interest, Ian regularly changes the wines on offer, provides tasting notes, and features unusual wines.

Since becoming a mother, Jacquie Pern, manager of the Star Inn at Harome in North Yorkshire, appreciates the family-friendly touches of some hotels and restaurants. Like Hambleton Hall on Rutland Water, where a kettle and nappy sacks are available in the bathroom.

Restaurant gross profit was increased 4% by adding supplements to some dishes to extend the table d'hôte menu. 'The idea came when we were eating out. It shows the importance of keeping eyes and ears open to what others are doing,' adds Don Birch, partner of the Beechwood Hotel in North Walsham, Norfolk.

A pig roaster means Daisy Chain Catering can offer outdoor barbecues to provide that extra special wedding reception, and bring interest to other outdoor events. Fiona Wisher used a cash prize she won to purchase the roaster.

A tearoom encourages customers to hand-finish their selection of cakes and pastries using a DIY kit of piping bags filled with cream and coloured fondants, trimmings such as ground nuts, glacé fruit, sugar strands, and a pair of tweezers. Everyone loves the idea and the piping bags are very popular for writing messages of affection between Bambi-eyed couples.

KING OF THE CASTLE 36

COMMONS TOUCH 54
We follow executive chef David Dorricott as he masterminds the 900th anniversary banquet held recently in Westminster Hall

PICKLE PER
Michelin-star Bramley offers in creating chutneys that carry a massive

Food, Drink and Equipment
SITE READING
Temporary kitchens can solve many problems, even on board an aircraft

A restaurant has set itself up as an informal introduction agency for the love-starved. On each table is a book with details of those looking for companionship, the results of questionnaires placed discreetly around the restaurant. No charge is made for entries in the contact book. From this, the restaurant arranges blind dinner-dates. There is no formal vetting process. The restaurateur relies on the integrity of customers.

Look at the local scene

Focus on events and developments that affect businesses and the lives of people around you. How is the local economy changing? What new housing, office and industrial developments are planned? Are businesses closing? What changes to the road and other transportation networks have taken place or are planned?

Getting reliable information – to confirm or dismiss local gossip or a speculative press report – may require visits to planning offices, and enquiries to one of the enterprise or advisory agents that help businesses in your area. Membership of locally-based organisations and groups is a valuable way of keeping abreast with (and, sometimes, influencing) developments.

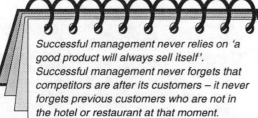

Successful management never relies on 'a good product will always sell itself'. Successful management never forgets that competitors are after its customers – it never forgets previous customers who are not in the hotel or restaurant at that moment.

Melvyn Greene, in Viewpoint, *Caterer & Hotelkeeper*

Local attractions

After learning of an initiative by his local tourist office to attract Dutch visitors to the area on walking holidays, Colin Hillyard, proprietor of the Priory Hotel in Louth, Lincolnshire has set up links with the office.

Speyside's whisky festival brings thousands to the area to celebrate the dram and the many traditions associated with it. A packed programme of events includes tastings tutored by whisky writers and industry experts, nosing competitions, the chance to take part in cask raising and planting, and cookery demonstrations.

Innovation with menus and a love of cricket help attract customers to the Griffings Head in Chillenden, Kent. Tenants Jerry and Karen Copestake have made their pub a cricketers' venue and were instrumental in setting up the local cricket team.

With the shooting season in full flow, Kevin Draper saw an opportunity for the Royal Oak to become better known among the affluent set who descend on Exmoor National Park during this time. But in negotiations to secure 10 bed nights for the season from one of the sporting agencies, he was told his prices for single occupancy might not appear expensive enough. So Draper came up with a dinner, bed and breakfast package including unlimited drinks except wine.

Being tucked away down a rural lane on the outskirts of Belfast has not proved a setback for restaurateurs Brian and Raymond McMillan. The brothers get regular bookings from many local groups including the football team and estimate that at least 30% of trade is repeat. Monthly theme evenings have proved popular, promoted by word of mouth and an announcement on the foot of each menu. There's no outlay on advertising.

Look at national trends

Your business is part of a much larger marketplace, where the consumer is influenced by fashion, the ups and downs of the British, European and world economies, natural and man-made disasters, threats to security, wars and other events. The effect of these can be quickly apparent, as it was on burger bars and restaurants specialising in beef dishes during the BSE crises.

Some changes are more gradual, such as the increase in the elderly population which has opened up a big market for many hotels and other accommodation providers, pubs and restaurants.

A pub which combines a distinctive, personal welcome with high standards of service and comfort, can fill the gap between guesthouse and hotel, appealing to business travellers on company expenses or self-employed, visitors to local events or attractions, house-hunters, UK holiday-makers touring or taking a short break, and overseas visitors.

They want character and personality in the licensee and staff, cleanliness, individuality, en-suite rooms and good breakfasts. A reasonable choice for an evening meal, friendly bars, preferably with local customers drinking local ales, credit card facilities and value for money, are also important.

Michael Sargent in *Caterer & Hotelkeeper*

Retired early, eat out more

The average age of the population is increasing, people retire earlier, live longer, and eat out more. By 2031, according to market researchers Key Note, well over half the UK adult population will be aged 45 or older.

What this market wants is a return to simple values such as good service, politeness, cleanliness, value for money and to be looked after. They have more time for pleasure activities.

Caterer & Hotelkeeper

The singles market

Many single people feel they are ignored, treated as second-class citizens and made to pay extortionate supplements. They resent the attitude from serving and front-of-house staff: 'how come you are on your own?'

To attract the singles market:

- train staff to be welcoming and receptive, and so help create an atmosphere of comfort and safety
- offer generously proportioned single rooms, with attractive ambience, and complimentary upgrades to double rooms when available
- organise a structure of activities, without guests feeling they are being coerced into participating
- provide informal, family-hotel service to help break the ice, with a host who can change a party of polite strangers into a lively group
- decide which group to target: those from their late 20s to late 50s, those aged 60 and over, lone parents with children – but remember that living and holidaying alone is not restricted to a social group or profession.

7.1.93

Caterer & Hotelkeeper, Gillian Jenner

Market your business

3 Target extra business

Be practical and a realist. Whatever your level of enthusiasm to go after all that untapped potential business, you cannot afford to devote unlimited time and resources to marketing. Instead, effort wants to be directed at the activities and the markets likely to generate results fairly quickly and in the most cost-effective way. Ideally, too, you want more business at those times you have the capacity and staff to deal with it. Nor should the extra business antagonise those regular customers you wish to keep.

Identify your business pattern

Statistics offer an objective way to track the ups and downs in your business. For example, you can compare the number of meals served, or bedrooms occupied with the previous week, month or year. You can identify variations by day of the week. You can monitor what region or country customers come from, how they travel, the average length of stay and average spend, as well as the popularity of individual dishes and drinks, and the number of people in each party.

Balance the amount of information against the effort involved in collecting and analysing it, and its potential use. If you are changing the design of your registration form, or buying a new cash till, a computer or software, consider how it can improve the scope and quality of your marketing information.

The aim is to identify the periods – these might be particular sessions, days of the week, or times of the year – when you would benefit from extra business. What customer groups are most likely to be attracted in greater numbers? What methods can be considered to reach those potential customers?

Patterns and trends

'There are many things to consider when changing the menu' says Mark Jones, retail brands operations director responsible for Exchange Bar Diners, the American-themed restaurants. 'We react to feedback from customers through comment cards and market research, we look at what our customers are doing, and we talk to our suppliers to discover what is new and selling well.'

'Market trends are a major consideration', says Jones. 'We look at what people are eating, such as the preference for chicken over beef. Then there is how they are eating – more emphasis on grazing, with customers sharing a selection of dishes in the centre of the table, instead of ordering three formal courses.'

'Lastly, we look at who is eating – although four is still the most popular number of people taking a table, there is a gradual increase in the size of each party.'

16.9.93

Caterer & Hotelkeeper

All things to all people

Ostrich, kangaroo or springbok feature on the menu at The Vine, a village pub in Cumnor. 'The pub was known for good food in the past, so I had to think about another marketing strategy,' explains landlord Robert Patterson.

Such a pub needs to be all things to all people. At one end is the 'local' with a pool table, fruit machines and villagers having a drink. In the conservatory, the garden room and, in the summer, the garden itself are young couples and retired folk enjoying an evening meal. At lunchtime, the business set drive four miles from Oxford to sample the unusual fare.

The local clientele is boosted by the 10 or so guesthouses in the vicinity. Patterson estimates he gets between 50% and 75% of the B&B customers for either lunch or dinner.

There is a no-booking policy for the restaurant, expect for customers coming from far away specifically for a meal. 'This is a village pub that does good food – not a restaurant pub.'

16.10.97

Caterer & Hotelkeeper, Sara Guild

Encourage repeat business

Present and past customers already know something about your business and what it offers them. That gives you a strong advantage. But their custom cannot be taken for granted. Even some of the country's top retailers, who are household names, have got into difficulties by losing touch with their customers.

Maintaining the quality of what you offer is crucial. A glich in service, poorly presented staff, a complaint mishandled ... any bad experience is likely to put off the customer at the receiving end.

Falling behind what competitors offer and/or changing customer expectations, in levels of comfort or service or range of products or prices charged, has a similar result. The time scale is longer, and you could miss the danger signs until quite late in the process, when it is significantly harder to correct the damage.

You may have regulars who come in every day. A more typical regular customer, however, needs timely reminders of the excellence of what you offer. When they get all manner of communications from competitors, they might feel you are taking their custom for granted, or not showing your appreciation if there is never anything from you. What they really value is your remembering birthdays, significant occasions and events.

Space guarantee wins loyal local trade

Three years visiting over 300 hospitality businesses throughout the UK helped Paul Whittome identify what would make his new business Hoste Arms, Burnham Market successful. Paul fosters a culture of accountability among his staff, with a monthly bonus as an incentive. To create a personal atmosphere, he circulates the dining areas to talk to customers. More controversially, 20 out of the 135 seats in the restaurant are automatically reserved for locals, even in the peak season. Thanks to this policy of encouraging locals, trade during winter is well above the average for the area. In February, for example, it was two-thirds of the peak summer month compared to one-quarter at other places.

1.10.98

Caterer & Hotelkeeper, Jenny Webster

Word spreads

'Regulars know that if they book a room they are going to get a reasonable size one, even if they are on their own,' says Thomas Noblette, manager. About 30% of business at the Langdale Chase hotel in Windermere now comes from single visitors, many of whom have just lost a partner, parent or child. Noblette accepts that selling to a single person means less profit during the summer, but he wins in the winter, smoothing the variation in occupancy levels. This winter he aims for 60% occupancy.

8.8.96

Caterer & Hotelkeeper, Jenny Webster

Birthday wishes

To help reposition Tummies bistro in Cippenham, near Slough, as a 'venue for that special occasion', owner Claude Mariaux compiled the birthdays of all customers on a database. She sends a card two weeks in advance of a birthday, offering an incentive, such as a small cake, to celebrate at Tummies.

19.1.95

Caterer & Hotelkeeper, Jenny Webster

Get recommendations

Word-of-mouth recommendation is hard to beat in terms of marketing effectiveness. People place great store on the judgement of those they know and share similar tastes and expectations with.

You have to earn a recommendation. By consistently pleasing your customers. By giving that special personal touch that marks your business out. And by taking swift action to put things right when there is a disappointment, because something has gone wrong, or customers put their own interpretation on the recommendation. 'Marvellous food' to one person may mean burger, chips and salad, not the more imaginative dishes which the person making the original recommendation so much enjoyed.

Some small hospitality businesses thrive on repeat custom and recommendations, and do no marketing. If you wish to follow this example, consider how long it may take to enjoy a worthwhile financial return. And what of those new customers who might be attracted by direct mail, news stories in the media, or some other means? New customers with the potential to be satisfied, to return and to recommend you.

Courting local goodwill

To court the local business community, an Italian cheese and wine tasting is being organised for January. Inviting corporate clients for a complimentary evening the previous year had cost Beechwood hotel £150, and helped create goodwill locally. An exhibition of a local artist's work may be combined with this year's event. Don Birch wants to get the invitations dropping through letter boxes when everyone is depressed after Christmas.

12.9.96

Caterer & Hotelkeeper, Linda Fox

Word of mouth

On setting up her mobile sandwich shop, Amanda Sainsbury made a three-year business plan. Within the first year, she achieved her end target, a turnover of £96,000. This was largely due to winning a contract to cater for 200 workmen at a site on the M4. Offering a range of quality sandwiches, cold savouries, salads, home-made cakes and biscuits and fresh fruit, with an emphasis on healthy eating (fried bread and chips is a once-a-month treat), she quickly built up a name for herself. Workmen tell her where new construction sites are located.

Amanda puts her success down to her commitment to turn up every day with a smile on her face, 'regardless of weather conditions, or any other of life's little hazards.'

23.1.97

Janet Harmer reporting on the 1997 winners of *Caterer & Hotelkeeper's* Peacock Awards

You cannot rely solely on word of mouth. Such publicity is essential but needs supplementing. It may fill the peaks but rarely the troughs. The total number of regulars who use you is not a fixed number. Some move out of the area, lose or change jobs, or read the publicity of competitors. You have to sell systematically to regulars and to people who have not used you.

Melvyn Greene, writing in *Caterer & Hotelkeeper*

Build a reputation

Those who work for you, and those you buy goods and services from, especially local suppliers, also contribute to the sort of reputation you enjoy. They may themselves become customers, and each has a circle of friends, family and other contacts who might ask where is good to eat, drink or stay.

Other influencers that impact directly and indirectly on how your business is perceived include:

- in the travel trade and tourism industry: those who can direct customers to your business

- journalists, editors and others in the local media: how they deal with incidents involving your business, and how responsive they are to requests for publicity for special events and other newsworthy items

- among fellow hospitality operators: who can recommend customers to you when they are fully booked, collaborate with joint marketing initiatives for the area, and pass on information about fraudulent credit cards, troublesome customers, etc.

Learning from failure

A contract where the restaurant (housed in a stunning room) was the prime attraction in the building lost the Digby Trout Restaurant £250,000. The entrance to the York Assembly Rooms was intimidating, customers had to come through two sets of doors to get in. And being a national monument, nothing could be done through better signage.

In spite of similar limitations, the company's venture at the Ashmolean museum in Oxford has been a happier story. 'The crucial elements for our success here are the cachet of being part of such an august body, which brings in the right sort of customer; the quality of the visitors the museum attracts; and the function business coming from the university, which has a knock-on effect as our reputation spreads,' explains Digby Trout. 'It is vital to be clear what you are good at when you operate in a niche market.'

6.2.97

Caterer & Hotelkeeper, Alan Sutton

Flowers say 'We care'

Every summer, tubs, hanging baskets and old milk churns brim with flowers outside the Nut Tree Inn in Murcott, Oxfordshire. 'There is little through traffic on this road, but no one could pass without taking notice and registering that we care. That is an important message for our regulars too', says Gordon Evans.

31.3.94

Caterer & Hotelkeeper, Jenny Webster

Do not try to be all things to all people. Concentrate on the things you do best, then provide them enthusiastically to the selected target groups with whom you are most comfortable.

Michael Sargent, *Caterer & Hotelkeeper*

Attract new customers

Follow a few straightforward, well tried, rules to maximise your success rate and avoid the pitfalls.

1 Focus on the market

Get the clearest possible picture of whom your message is aimed at. Retired couples for out-of-season breaks. Youngsters for disco evenings. Local businesses for conferences. Walkers using the national trail which passes nearby. Families on a day's outing by car. Non-smokers. Vegetarians. Tourists from mainland Europe.

Refer to the process you went through earlier, in identifying main customer groups and potential new markets. The list of target markets need not be long, and the more specific it is the better. For example, if your area has most visitors from the Netherlands, you should probably focus on attracting more of them rather than the 'Tourists from mainland Europe' on your original list.

Don't be concerned if your target markets appear to lack glamour. It's what will work for you that matters. The realities of your business are what should be reflected.

Rural appeal of good food

'In a rural area like this, we decided a restaurant has greater earning potential than beds, and is more likely to attract repeat business,' explained Charlie and Frances Baker-Vilain. 'Research indicated we would have almost no competition in the middle to top-end restaurant market within a 10–15 mile radius.' To get people talking about the new focus on food – Stretton Hall had been a hotel with a dining room – a special value Sunday lunch was offered.

8.10.98

Caterer & Hotelkeeper, Rosalind Mullen

Balancing on the tightrope

'Families are our core business', says Mark Jones, speaking about Exchange Bar Diners, the American-themed restaurants. 'But we have to tread the tightrope carefully so as not to become too child-orientated and drive away the young trendies who help provide a more adult party atmosphere on Friday and Saturday nights.'

16.9.93

Caterer & Hotelkeeper

Tex-Mex attracts American air crew

With a new Tex Mex menu, and more sittings, John Elworthy was soon filling The Chequers, a pub in Eriswell, with air crews and their families from the nearby American Air Force base. A special event programme added to the appeal. These included mystery and suspense nights, based on spooky local history.

28.9.98

Publican, announcing the award Marketing Pub of the Year to The Chequers

2 Decide what will attract that market

Having refined your list, you can begin to concentrate on what appeals to each market. For the Dutch, it might be the varied and beautiful landscape, quiet roads, and ease of access.

Take the customers' viewpoint. Being amongst young trendy, fashion-aware people for an evening's entertainment may not appeal to you, but is it important to your nightclub clientele?

The rapid expansion of roadside lodges, hotels and motels has been based on the appeal of convenient location, quality standard product (people know exactly what comfort and facilities to expect), value for money (especially when two or more can share the same bedroom), and ease of booking (with a national booking centre, and referral systems so that alternatives are offered when the first choice is fully booked). Of more recent appeal, aimed at the business travellers segment of the market, are modem terminals so that information can be downloaded or transferred from portable computers in guests' bedrooms.

Notice what does not appear on this list: food, personal service, luxury, quiet location, outstanding views, swimming pool, leisure facilities.

Inns with appeal (to the over 55)

- location is crucial: the drive to the inn is an important part of the outing, scenic country and quiet roads are ideal
- older people are often prepared to drive 10 to 15 miles, but convenient parking is essential
- the setting should appeal, e.g. facing village green, with beautiful views; exceptional pubs in small country towns may qualify
- good external and internal appearance, style says 'quality, high degree of professionalism'
- furniture, fittings, decor and lighting suit the setting: excessive theming or regimented lines of furniture from catalogues not appreciated
- high standards of hygiene and cleanliness, not least in the lavatories
- relaxed, informal ambience, with good temperature control, open fires in winter a plus
- not smoky, because most of this age group have been serious smokers in the past and now have the convictions of the converted
- conviviality, the feeling of being among friends
- no music: this generation does not take readily to other people's choice of music; the best background is the buzz of conversation, clink of glasses and rattle of cutlery
- personal attention: to be welcomed quickly and courteously; the manager is the key: he or she stamps personality on the inn and ensures that his or her style of service is reflected by the staff
- quality of service matters hugely, consistency and reliability, not servility
- drinking is not the prime aim of the visit, and one person from each group will usually be driving
- primarily lunch time visits, menu which offers dishes that are sufficiently out of the ordinary to tempt customers who eat out frequently
- genuine home-made dishes are recognised and appreciated, but the style must not be too heavy
- older customers are often not big eaters; one or two courses is the general rule for a main meal
- fish and shellfish-based dishes are popular, puddings can tempt, particularly with those that have chosen a low cholesterol first course
- not in a hurry and happy to linger over coffee
- expect smooth service, e.g. tables kept clear, bill brought promptly when requested, credit card facilities offered
- highly aware of the value of money.

20.4.95

Caterer & Hotelkeeper, Michael Sargent and Tony Lyle

3 What makes your business special?

Set yourself apart from the competition. Find a way of expressing those things you do much better than anyone else, or which make your position uniquely placed to meet the customers' needs.

Running a small business already gives you advantages over the large, company-owned competitors and big groups:

- the appeal of a personal welcome, customers are treated as friends (some may become friends)

- continuity: in the larger companies, senior personnel and serving staff tend to move on more frequently than in small, family-run businesses

- the time, opportunity and motivation to treat customers as individuals

- the lack of standardisation, with genuine character to the decor, food, furnishings and fittings

- a product which reflects its location, rather than some national formula

- greater flexibility to respond to different needs, as you are not bound by head office rules or procedures

- someone on the spot to take responsibility when things go wrong, or a decision has to be made.

French lesson

Local produce is largely ignored in the UK, while the French make it a unique selling point. In St Malo in Brittany, for example, small family owned restaurants feature dishes using apples and cider from Fouesnant, tuna and crab straight from the nearby auctions, oysters, clams, whelks, prawns, shrimps, cockles and mussels from nearby beds, and biscuits and cakes made from ancient local recipes.

1.10.98

Caterer & Hotelkeeper, Roger Wilsher

Royally distinctive

To be distinctive was the only way to stand out in Harrogate's crowded, mid-range market, Alison Hartwell realised. So she worked on the royal theme. Pictures of the Queen cram the walls. The Oriental Bar is choc-a-bloc with chinoiserie: lacquered furniture, paintings, sculpture. The snug besides the entrance hall is crowded with cats: china cats, painted cats, fabric cats.

At the same time, Hartwell started a programme of promotions. For August, a slow month for corporate business, she offered a special B&B rate through the tourist information office. The cost was minimal: printing one leaflet.

September's promotion, aimed at guests who've come on weekend breaks, offers them a return special rate of two nights for the price of one.

9.96

The Restaurant Business

No children

No children under 12 are accepted at the Hope End in Ledbury. 'The reason', proprietor Patricia Hegarty, explains 'is because people come here to relax and often to get away from their own children. We are in a very quiet position and there's not a great deal for children to do. We don't have televisions. We've also got large ponds in the grounds which wouldn't be suitable for young children.'

31.3.94

Caterer & Hotelkeeper, Jenny Webster

4 Review your options

Nothing may persuade you to walk the streets with a billboard, but it can be hard to say 'no' to the secretary of the local football club or Women's Institute, who asks for your support with a small advertisement in their anniversary issue magazine. Between these extremes, there are many methods you can choose from to market your business, including the newer developments: email and a website on the Internet. The cost, ease of arranging and suitability vary considerably. Your choice should build on the work you have already done in identifying who you want to target, what message is likely to appeal, and the results of using these and similar marketing methods in the past.

Corporate identity

A corporate identity is established through the use of certain typefaces and sizes for your business name, generally a logo and the colours and design of printed material. By these means you send a message that this is your business, distinguished from all others.

Carry the same theme through all your printed material including letterheads, business cards, menus, wine lists, leaflets and brochures, on signs, in advertisements, and, if you have the resources for such items: badged crockery, cutlery and glassware, personalised uniforms, name tags, towels, napkins, place and drink mats. Continuity in appearance creates confidence and unity. Each item reinforces the other. Recognition is assisted.

Brief printers, designers and anyone else involved in the production of such items, on your requirements for typefaces, logo, colours and design. If they suggest changes or present different ideas, test them first for their potential impact on the overall identity you have created.

How not to do it

The 45-seater Bench restaurant in Middlesbrough was busy on its opening day. But the restaurant's crime theme and owner Sean Wilkin's decor featuring notorious criminals, caused an uproar in the local media. A former chief superintendent of Durham police, Lord Mackenzie, called upon diners to boycott the new restaurant.

17.9.98

Caterer & Hotelkeeper

Success is that combination of spaces, colours, furnishings, lighting, temperature, air quality and presentation which adds up to 'ambience', a quality we recognise and appreciate but cannot always define.

Look at the whole pub, inside and out, continually checking that the image you wish to present is being delivered to your customers and potential customers consistently and reliably. It's easy to lose a customer and extremely hard to get that customer back again.

Image does not stop at the pub itself: how you and your staff present yourselves and the quality of service you give are vital. Staff need to know and understand the marketing objectives and be trained to help meet them.

This image extends to printed material: business cards, letterheads, invoices, posters – everything should have a consistency which is readily identifiable. One slapdash item can do as much damage as a poorly presented meal.

Michael Sargent, *Caterer & Hotelkeeper*

Signage

Imagine that you are approaching and entering your premises for the first time, or ask a friend to do this. Is it easy to find? Consider the different ways in which people arrive, and the directions from which they can come. Is it clear where to park, which way to go to enter the building? Are disabled people given help? Once in the building, is it easy to find the toilets, the lounge, restaurant, bars, bedrooms, etc.?

Signs should tell people what your business is, give a welcome and a flavour of what customers can expect. They can also announce what is available: quiz night tonight. People should not be surprised – check back on those casual remarks and conversations you have overhead, and what people have said directly to you or your staff – that they didn't know you did bed & breakfast, have a liquor licence, serve take-aways.

Too many signs about who is not welcome, what behaviour or dress is forbidden, indicate bossiness. Too many signs with a direct selling message can become confusing and have little impact.

When considering new external signs, check the need for planning approval from your local authority, the owners of the land or buildings (if not you), and any organisations involved because of the building's historic or architectural interest.

Signs give wrong image

Among the weaknesses consultants identified at Cross Keys, a restaurant featured in *Caterer & Hotelkeeper's* Lifesavers' series (see pages 5 and 9), were poor external signs. The simple lettering on a cream background did not conjure up the image of a cosy country restaurant – a pictorial sign was suggested. Other weaknesses and the consultant's recommendations for dealing with them were:

- guests were confused by the choice of where and what they can order – physical differences between the environment and atmosphere and pricing policy and the level of service between the bar and restaurant needed to be made clearer
- value for money: customers acknowledged that the quality of food was significantly better than the competition, but prices were too high – the menu should be redesigned and the number of items reduced
- a visual conflict between the modern restaurant extension and the original parts of the building – the new roof tiles and brick walls should be treated to encourage the growth of lichens and moss, and climbing plants and window boxes used to give the exterior a country cottage look
- the colour scheme of blue upholstery fabric and table cloths with white walls, gave a rather chilly and uninviting overall effect – the walls should be repainted with a pink emulsion, the table covers changed to pink, and more appropriate pictures selected for the walls
- less than half the customers rated the service as friendly and helpful – the husband or wife should take a front-of-house role to bring a personal touch. Alternatively, the present dining room supervisor should be trained to the correct standard, or a suitably qualified person brought in.

22.10.92

Caterer & Hotelkeeper, Catey Hillier

In-house selling

Each telephone or face-to-face contact customers have with you or your staff, is a chance to sell:

- *an enquiry:* describe facilities, send a brochure, offer to make a booking

- *on arrival:* offer to book a table for dinner, describe the dish of the day, offer to bring the wine list

- *when ordering:* suggest and describe dishes and drinks, respond to clues: 'as you are celebrating, what about the ...', offer room upgrades at 'only £X extra', tell them about special offers

- *when clearing during a meal:* suggest a glass of dessert wine with the sweet

- *on departure:* offer to send them details of upcoming events.

Handle such selling opportunities in a way which suits your personality. See it as helping customers to make a more informed choice, confident in their decision. Be sensitive to those who do not want help. Nothing is gained by showing up lack of knowledge.

Assist your staff to recognise the appropriate times to sell, and how to put across the benefits. Help them to speak from experience, because they are proud of your facilities, know what the dishes of the day are and how they have been made, and when they are asked a question they can't answer, take the trouble to find and convey the information.

Consider how you reward staff. The use of an incentive scheme, with increases in sales leading to additional pay or a bonus, is a powerful motivator.

On the role your staff can play

- be smart in appearance
- keep work areas clean, tidy and safe
- show a pleasant, friendly attitude
- attend to customers promptly, both in person and telephone callers
- use customers' names where known
- put customers at their ease
- learn customers' names, and their likes and dislikes
- know what services and products you offer
- be able to advise on local facilities, transport, etc.
- if unable to answer guests' questions, find someone who can
- describe facilities and services in a helpful way
- anticipate problems and act quickly to put matters right
- deal effectively with complaints
- use appropriate body language, and respond to guests' body language
- show a helpful attitude to other members of staff

When you receive a telephone enquiry for a brochure and tariff, don't just send these items to the caller.

Firstly ask some questions. Ask the caller the type of room, when they are planning to come, how many people, what are their interests? This shouldn't take too long and shows you are really interested in them.

Then stress one sales point, an advantage, such as 'Our swimming pool has a safe area for young children.'

Ask if you can make a provisional booking and hold this for them for, say, four days. Some people will say no. A lot will say yes. Offering to make a provisional booking is not a 'hard sell' but simply a service. You have to word it tactfully; for example 'We do have rooms available for that date at the moment, but we are filling up fast.'

Melvyn Greene, writing in *The Restaurant Business*

Face-to-face or direct selling

You do this, even if you do not recognise it as selling, when you discuss arrangements for special events with customers, and show people your bedrooms and meetings rooms. You already have the potential customer's interest, you are in a two-way dialogue so you can respond to the person's reactions, as well as lead the discussion. To get the full benefits of these advantages:

- be prepared: with an understanding of the potential customer's needs, and all relevant information ready to hand

- be hospitable: punctual, provide a comfortable place to meet, offer refreshments, get a colleague to answer the phone and prevent other interruptions, show the facilities, introduce key personnel, put the 'prospect' at ease

- be sensitive and respond as appropriate to concerns, reservations and lack of enthusiasm, as well as indications of interest, clues to needs, and questions

- gain and retain interest, express what you are offering in such a way that they come across as benefits to the person

- judge when to invite agreement of the deal

- sum up what has been agreed, confirm prices, clarify the next stages, e.g. make a provisional booking, choose the final menu.

Afternoon tea invite

The pub's relationship with the local Chamber of Commerce has been particularly profitable. Edwin and Trudy Cheeseman invited 100 local businesses to an afternoon tea, which cost them roughly £200 to host. Less than a week later, the Carrington Arms in Moulsoe, Buckinghamshire, was already receiving new business from at least 10 of these companies.

10.7.97

Caterer & Hotelkeeper, Linda Fox

Wedding fair attracts

To get people to attend, James Main of Wortley House in Scunthorpe, ran a free draw. The prize: a wedding reception at the hotel for 75 people. The day was publicised in local newspapers and through mailshots to everyone who had made a wedding booking or enquiry. It was an open-door policy on the day.

To offset the cost of the prize, Main asked the hotel's suppliers to donate food and drink. Exhibitors at the wedding fair were also asked to donate prizes. Quickly, it grew into a basic wedding package, including reception, dress, morning suit hire, hair dressing, photography, cars, two rings, video, flowers, disco, chocolates and even balloons for the tables.

When Main invites local providers of wedding services to exhibit, he is careful to balance their wish for exclusivity with the aim of giving the public a choice. Consequently no more than two dressmakers, photographers, car hire businesses, florists, etc. have stands at the same fair.

His advice is to get money up front from exhibitors, have plenty of helpful staff mixing with visitors, and have a star attraction such as a raffle prize or fashion draw.

Caterer & Hotelkeeper (adapted)

Merchandising

Consider how shelf, counter, window and buffet table arrangements can be made more appealing to customers. Identify the best selling positions – those people tend to look at as they enter the room, sit at a table, stand at the bar – and use them to display products on which you make a good profit, or which you wish particularly to promote.

Follow the example of supermarkets and shops, with use of location, lighting, colour, shape and aromas (fresh coffee, freshly-baked bread). Where people sometimes wait to sign in, or to order a drink, for example, position information on special offers, postcards, snacks, souvenirs, home-made jams, guide books and similar impulse sellers.

Some suppliers, to help you promote their products or certain brands, offer a range of practical, novelty or gimmicky items. These include beer mats, coasters and menu holders, posters, window stickers, table tent cards, display panels and stands, badged glassware and crockery, pens, calendars, key holders, even furry animals. You may get them free, perhaps linked to a minimum order value with that supplier, or at a subsidised price. They may be a national promotion organised by a food or drink marketing organisation.

Ask sales representatives what they can provide. Be ready to negotiate when considering what prominence to give their products on shelves behind the bar or service counter.

Gifts to attract

Attracting passing family trade is key to the success of Lincoln-based Jay-Dees restaurants. To draw people in from the street, managing director John Downs regularly comes up with a novel gift appropriate to the season.

This summer, his entire stock of windmills on sticks was quickly snapped up by local children. At Christmas, giving furry bugs to young customers, and calendar cards to adults also proved popular. But the children's sunglasses he bought for last summer are still stacked in a storeroom. 'It's important to make offers that have a high perceived value, but a low actual cost,' says John.

24.9.98

Caterer & Hotelkeeper

Your menu is an advertisement. And what's the most important thing about an advertisement? The headline. An effective headline encapsulates the most important customer benefit you have to offer. 'Menu' is not a headline, nor is 'Grand Hotel Restaurant'. Use something equivalent to 'British Airways – the world's favourite airline'.

Display the menu, well lit, behind non-reflective glass, where it will attract the passer-by. To attract people, they have to know that what's on offer is attractive. Put a professional photograph of your nice restaurant alongside the menu.

Derek Taylor in *Hotel & Catering Business*

Guide books

To these, many people turn for ideas, information and opinions on where to eat, drink or stay. Some guides employ full or part-time inspectors, returning a number of times incognito before you are graded and listed in the next edition. Regular inspections follow to monitor standards. No payment is involved, the publishers make their money from sales of the guide, and perhaps sponsorship by a supplier.

Other guides enforce certain minimum standards before offering entry, but charge you a fee. The description and/or rating is in some cases the result of this inspection, or it may be based on customers' reports, or a mixture. With yet other guides, you write the description, so it is more comparable to advertising, except that the publication is devoted to promoting similar businesses to yours.

Before paying for such a guide entry – typically, the money is demanded before publication – do check out the organisation carefully. Visit bookshops and tourist offices to see copies for yourself, judge their potential value and usefulness to customers, and compare them to the others available.

If you are invited to participate in a new guide, ignore the flattery and tempting terms for advance payment. Ask for evidence of financial soundness. Seek the advice of your trade or professional association. Many hoteliers and restaurateurs have paid for entries in guides that prove to be hoaxes, or for some other reason fail to be published, or to be distributed in the way and quantities originally claimed.

Be warned

Offered a certificate of merit by the publisher of a café guide, David Buick of the Upstairs Downstairs café in Arscaig on the shore of Loch Shin, was over the moon. Buick sent off the money, but heard nothing. Leyton CID, who were investigating the fraud, received over 400 similar stories. An accommodation address had been used, from which mail was forwarded overseas.

The Restaurant Business

Power of reviews

Listings and reviews in directories and guide books are the most persuasive publicity of all, says Michael Vaughan, proprietor of the Old Rectory in Llansantffraid, North Wales. Good write-ups in several guides are particularly valuable because tourists usually cross reference before making their choice.

The Old Rectory attracts cultured, independent types looking for a low-key hotel with high standards. Its peaceful, private location, in two acres of formal gardens with dramatic views, is a powerful draw. Half of the guests book on the strength of the hotel's reputation for food.

The Vaughans found advertising in the national papers, where even a miniscule classified ad costs hundreds, yielded no business.

2.94

Hotel & Restaurant, Emily Kindersley

Join or form a consortium

Consortia bring you together with similar independent businesses, to share the advantages of a stronger market presence. They range from small locally-based groups which collaborate on promoting the town or area to large national and international organisations with powerful branding and huge resources including a reservations network. There may also be purchasing arrangements, so you get a discount from certain suppliers, training providers and advertising media.

Generally you pay an annual fee, linked to the size of business. There may be a joining fee. With some, commission has to be paid on bookings. Check what other extra costs you may face, what the benefits are, the criteria for joining, and the notice to be given if you leave the consortium. Speak to a range of existing members, to check their satisfaction and what they see as the main advantages and any disadvantages. (The Hotel & Catering International Management Association publishes a directory of hotel consortia. Trade bodies can also help, see opposite page.)

Collaboration pays

With many visitors to cities like Oxford, Cambridge and York, spending at most a few hours before they go on to their next destination, hoteliers have had to work hard to encourage longer stays.

In Oxford, Michael Thompson, manager of the Old Parsonage hotel, got together with other operators in the leisure sector to produce a quarterly newsletter to raise the profile of the city. It is mailed to travel agents and travel writers, in the UK and abroad.

In Cambridge, six hotels jointly promote short breaks. In York, the Three Cheers for York package includes supersaver return tickets for rail travellers and preferential B&B rates.

24.2.94

Caterer & Hotelkeeper, David Tarpey

Plant centre link brings mutual benefits

The Loch Fyne Oyster Bar in Elton near Peterborough produces a simple leaflet offering diners a discount at the nearby Bressingham Plant Centre, which in turn offers a discount to its customers for a meal at the Oyster Bar.

1.8.96

Caterer & Hotelkeeper, Michael Sargent

Equal status makes good food circle

Restaurateurs of Kinsale, Co Cork, have formed the Kinsale Good Food Circle: 'No one is at the top, and no one at the bottom.' Co-operation includes:

- staggering holidays, so that six of the 11 restaurants are always open
- anonymous annual inspection of members' restaurants
- joint marketing and advertising
- a referral system: 'if one restaurant is full, we never hesitate to recommend another'
- not getting involved in running anyone else's business, nor poaching staff.

The culmination of working together comes in an annual gourmet festival, when some 350 people visit Kinsale for four days of eating, drinking and entertainment.

26.9.96

Caterer & Hotelkeeper, Jenny Webster

Joining a marketing consortium

Joining a marketing consortium

- ❤ choose the consortium to suit your business
- ❤ be clear about the type of business you expect: no good if the consortium only produces business when you are already full
- ❤ be realistic about the benefits: membership is not a magic wand
- ❤ vital to get the right relationship from the beginning
- ❤ go to the HQ, meet the people who will be selling your product
- ❤ talk to current consortium members in similar situation to yours: ask about good and bad points, quality control
- ❤ look at the small print before you sign: may be financial penalties for breaking the contract early
- ❤ be prepared to take an active role, keep up with paperwork, go to regional meetings and AGMs, when asked for marketing material, e.g. photos, provide good quality material, invite central reservations or conference staff to see your business

Register with the tourist board

For establishments which offer accommodation, this brings the benefit of recognition by a national organisation, having met certain minimum standards. Through the inspection and grading scheme, members are able to publicly demonstrate the level of facilities and quality of service offered. Customers know broadly what to expect from the number of stars or other symbol awarded.

Members can advertise in the various tourist board publications and guides, and participate in trade and public promotions. Fees depend on the prestige and target audience of the venture.

ADDRESS BOOK

PROFESSIONAL BODIES

British Institute of Innkeeping
Park House, 24 Park Street, Camberley, Surrey
GU15 3PL
Tel: 01276 684449 Fax: 01276 23045
Email: membership@BII.org
Website: www.barzone.co.uk

Chartered Institute of Marketing
Moor Hall, Cookham, Maidenhead, Berks SL6 9QH
Tel: 01628 427500 Fax: 01628 427499
Email: marketing@cim.co.uk
Website: www.cim.co.uk

Hotel & Catering International Management
Association
191 Trinity Road, London SW17 7HN
Tel: 0181 672 4251 (020 8672 4251 from 22.4.00)
Fax: 0181 682 1707 (020 8682 1707 from 22.4.00)
Email: library@hcima.org.uk
Website: hcima.org.uk

Tourism Society
26 Chapter Street, London SW1P 4ND
Tel: 0171 834 0461 (020 7834 0461 from 22.4.00)
Fax: 0171 932 0238 (020 7932 0238 from 22.4.00)
Email: tour.soc@htinternet.com

TRADE BODIES

British Hospitality Association
Queens House, 55–56 Lincoln's Inn Fields, London
WC2A 3BH
Tel: 0171 404 7744 (020 7404 7744 from 22.4.00)
Fax: 0171 404 7799 (020 7404 7799 from 22.4.00)
Email: bha@bha.org.uk
Website: www.bha-online.org.uk

Hospitality Association of Northern Ireland
The Midland Building, Whitla Street, Belfast
BT15 1JP
Tel: 01232 351110 (028 9035 1110 from 22.4.00)
Fax: 01232 351509 (028 9035 1509 from 22.4.00)

Restaurant Association
Africa House, 64–78 Kingsway, London WC2B 6AH
Tel: 0171 831 8727 (020 7831 8727 from 22.4.00)
Fax: 0171 831 8703 (020 7831 8703 from 22.4.00)
Email: ragb@easynet.co.uk
Website: www.ragb.co.uk

NATIONAL TOURIST BODIES

English Tourism Council
Thames Council, Black's Road, London W6 9EL
Tel: 0181 846 9000 (020 8846 9000 from 22.4.00)
Fax: 0181 563 0302 (020 8563 0302 from 22.4.00)
Website: www.englishtourism.org.uk

Northern Ireland Tourist Board
St Anne's Court, 59 North Street, Belfast BT1 1NB
Tel: 01232 231221 (028 9023 1221 from 22.4.00)
Fax: 01232 240960 (028 9024 0960 from 22.4.00)
Email: general.enquiriesnitb@nics.gov.uk
Website: www.ni-tourism.com

Scottish Tourist Board
23 Ravelston Terrace, Edinburgh EH4 3EU
Tel: 0131 332 2433
Fax: 0131 332 4441
Email: info@stb.gov.uk
Website: www.holiday.scotland.net

Wales Tourist Board
Brunel House, 2 Fitzalan Road, Cardiff CF2 1UY
Tel: 01222 499909 (029 2049 9909 from 22.4.00)
Fax: 01222 485031 (029 2048 5031 from 22.4.00)
Email: info@tourism.wales.gov.uk
Website: www.tourism.wales.gov.uk

Public relations

How neighbours and local people regard your business can be crucial when you seek planning permission, a new licence, or renewal of an existing licence. Complaints about noise, parking, rubbish and other warnings that all is not well, need sensitive treatment and action to lessen the cause for complaint. Doing nothing will lose you vital allies and possibly create enemies.

Besides affecting your customer base, what people think of you influences how easy it is to recruit local staff, and the sort of response locals give to out-of-area visitors who ask where to eat, drink or stay. Ways to raise your profile include:

- organising or participating in charity events

- sponsoring, contributing to or taking part in local sports teams, arts and cultural events

- playing an active role in local organisations: as a school governor, councillor, chamber of trade member, etc.

The other aspect to public relations is media exposure. Get a good story in a newspaper or magazine, or on the radio or TV, and you bring your business to the attention of a wide audience, without the constraints or expense of advertising: people give more value to editorial than they do to advertising copy. A telephone call to the editor or a reporter may be sufficient, although it is more usual to send a press release and photograph. Wining and dining key contacts is another strategy. Travel writers and reviewers may expect to sample the whole package free, including accommodation.

Winning idea

A Valentine weekend with a difference: a Bentley Azure to keep. A photograph showing the luxury car (borrowed from a local dealer) outside the hotel was sent with the press release. Although there were no takers for the £199,000 package, it got Hellaby Hall Hotel in Rotherham plenty of editorial coverage, and brought in 200 customers over three days spending £25 on average for the special meal with flowers and music from the resident pianist.

9.96

The Restaurant Business

Involving local community

A good relationship with the local community is seen as vital to the success of the three hotels in Southwold, Suffolk which make up the Adnams group. Dudley Clarke, general manager, donates money each year to schools and local groups, and allows the town's shopkeepers to hold fashion shows and exhibitions in the hotels.

Annual events to draw in customers and locals include three gardening weekends, a Stout and Seafood Festival and a literary weekend. Recently an open day was held for townspeople to pass judgement on the seven refurbished garden rooms at the Swan.

Clarke encourages staff to participate in town life. A head chef is a member of the local lifeboat crew, and a hotel manager sits on the parish council. Clarke dresses up as the town's Father Christmas each year.

Clarke still gets the odd jibe from locals that the extra visitors make parking difficult.

30.4.98

Caterer & Hotelkeeper, Linda Fox

Ice hockey team waits for charity

Each year the local ice hockey team take over the waiting at Spagg's pizza and pasta restaurant, which fills with their supporters. Proprietor Tammy Mariaux donates the proceeds of a raffle and a generous proportion of the evening's takings to the NSPCC 'because both the restaurant and the ice hockey team are involved with children every day.'

Caterer & Hotelkeeper Reader Diaries

Swindlesham Hall
Moaning Newbridge NE1 4T
Tel: 01222 222222

PRESS RELEASE

- choose media and titles appropriate to your business, your story and your locality

- respect copy deadlines: telephone the recipients of your release first, to establish last date for information in the relevant issue

- use this call to find out name and position of the most appropriate person to direct the release to

- use letterhead paper (or head the paper with your business name, address and telephone number) and bold headline: press release

- type the release in double spacing, with generous margins (this makes it easier for the editor to amend)

- date the release: if the information is not to be published before a certain date, head 'embargoed until [date]'

- use an attention-catching headline (to make the editor think this is worthy of publication), which conveys the essence of the story in a few words

- write your story in the style of the paper(s)/magazine(s) you are aiming at

- begin with the most newsworthy information (in the first paragraph), to grab the editor's (and readers') attention

- keep the release short, ideally a single A4 page

- include a quote (from you or someone relevant to the story) where this will add human interest

- give contact name and telephone number or other appropriate information so readers can respond (e.g. to make a booking)

- put any necessary background information (e.g. number of rooms, opening times) at the end under 'Notes for editor' (these are single-spaced)

- end with 'More information is available from:' and give a contact name and phone number (this is for the editor to follow up)

- where appropriate, include a good photograph (black and white/colour depending on the paper/magazine); write the relevant information about the photograph (for when it becomes detached from the press release) on an adhesive label, and place the label on the reverse of the photo (don't write directly on the back of a photograph with a hard pen or pencil, or it will show through)

- follow up the release with a telephone call: be ready to be interviewed on the telephone and do not say anything which you would not wish to read in print

- at this stage offer further information, photographs, or an invitation to visit if the contact is interested

Advertising

You pay a publisher, agent or entrepreneur to convey your message in a newspaper, magazine, shop window or guide book, on a calendar, wall planner, poster or some other printed material. At your disposal is a potentially powerful combination of words, design, imagery and perhaps photographs. When the radio, cinema or television is the medium, sound and movement are also available.

The first aim is to gain the attention of potential customers – a quick glance through any magazine or newspaper will show the multiplicity of ways of doing this, and their relative success. You then want to create interest and generate desire – the subject partly does this, when combined with words and images that appeal to your target audience. Finally, you want to encourage a response. At the least this means a telephone number, usually an address plus other helpful information such as fax number, email and website addresses.

The costs reflect how many people are expected to read, see, receive, hear or watch the advertisement, the size or broadcast length of the advertisement, its design or production, and the prestige of the medium. Those selling advertisements try for the highest price they believe they can command. A card in a shop window may cost a matter of pence per week, while a TV advert costs many thousands with the maximum charges applying at peak viewing times. Colour advertisements in magazines and newspapers cost substantially more than black and white, because of the extra production costs and the greater appeal.

Presenting the guide to effective advertising

AIDA
attract Attention

Through design, use of graphics or photographs and/or strong headings and perhaps a border, your advert should stand out from those around it.

AIDA
create Interest

You've got the reader to look at the advert, now keep the person's attention by creating interest. Design and words again play a key role.

AIDA
generate Desire

Express what you want to sell as benefits to the reader. Use words which will appeal to the target audience, and keep them reading!

AIDA
stimulate Action

Get the reader to telephone, send for a brochure, visit. Make it clear what the reader has to do to buy or get more information. Encourage immediate response.

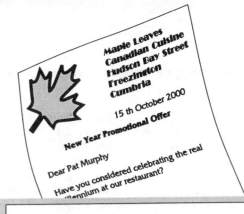

Maple Leaves
Canadian Cuisine
Hudson Bay Street
Freezington
Cumbria

15 th October 2000

New Year Promotional Offer

Dear Pat Murphy

Have you considered celebrating the real
millennium at our restaurant?

The Comely Arms
Buxom Beds

On crafting promotional messages

- aim to get reader's attention in the first 12 words or so
- concentrate on the features your customers want
- choose words which convey the benefits to customers: 'sell the sizzle not the steak'
- keep sentences, paragraphs and the message itself short
- focus on one or two selling messages, do not try to squeeze in too much information
- use headings to catch attention, emphasise main points, guide readers
- say what is special, and who says so, but don't over-praise your products
- appeal to reader's curiosity by asking questions, linking to local events
- use lots of 'you's, very few 'we's, 'I's or 'they's
- generally better to be informal, rather than formal in writing style
- be honest: do not attempt to portray an image that differs from reality
- have some way of encouraging the reader to respond, and establish clearly what you want the reader/receiver to do
- address direct mail letters by name, if names are unavailable, use 'Dear Neighbour', 'Dear Guest', 'Dear Party-lover', etc. (not the impersonal as in 'Dear Sir/Madam')
- include people but avoid model-like poses in photographs
- ask a friend or colleague to check for sense, impact and mistakes
- PS at end of a direct mail letter is an effective way of gaining attention

Dolly's Cafe
Special Sunday Lunch

Kids eat free with an adult
Pensioners half-price

Book first to avoid disappointment
Phone 01196 412214

The County Times

When advertising, remember that papers, magazines, radio and television programmes appeal to different audiences. To ensure your value for money there must be a match between the readers, listeners or viewers to your declared target markets. You must interest potential customers and spur them into action by your ad.

Read it from the customer's viewpoint – does it catch the eye, has it something to say, does it offer a benefit? And from your point of view, will it create business?

Good ads are a mixture of the correct medium and a strong, well-presented, selling message – get both right and your advertising can produce results.'

Michael Sargent, *Caterer & Hotelkeeper*

Direct mail

The postal service delivers your message to homes and/or businesses. For the addresses, you should use records of past customers and enquiries. You can search telephone, business and other directories and guides, the electoral register, or buy labels or a computer disc from a company specialising in direct mail lists. Alternatively, the post office will deliver your (unaddressed) material to every household on mail rounds of your choice. Newsagents, scout groups or enterprising (and fit!) individuals may also be willing to do this.

The more personal and professional your addressed envelope looks, the more likely it is to be opened:

- people feel they should pay attention to businesslike mail (recognised by the typed address or word-processed label used) as it might contain important information from their bank, pension company, etc., a bill which has to be paid, or a new credit card

- on the other hand, many people hate junk mail: envelopes addressed to the occupier or head of household, or with other clues that they are unsolicited, tend to go straight into the bin.

Having got them to open the envelope, if you can give the impression that this is a personal letter, you are more likely to hold their attention. Then the message and appearance of other contents, such as a brochure, can play their role.

Turnover tripled

A mail shot to 25,000 local homes increased turnover of an 80-seater restaurant in North Harrow threefold. Tony Bricknell-Webb, proprietor, arranged for the Post Office to deliver discount vouchers off a three-course meal to each home. The values of the vouchers (for parties of two, four and six) were chosen to match the size of tables at the restaurant, and subsequent bookings picked to maximise table occupancy.

23.7.92

Caterer & Hotelkeeper

Diner's club

Creating a club gives Stephen Ross, proprietor of the Olive Tree Restaurant in Bath a platform to tell regular diners about his various promotions and create business for the slower periods. Around 800 members receive a quarterly newsletter and details of bi-monthly special offers. Revenue has been boosted by 35 to 40%. The work of building and maintaining the database (which is computerised), writing the newsletter, printing and mailing is divided among the restaurant team.

20.5.93

Caterer & Hotelkeeper, Sandra Lawson and Alastair Stevenson

A message, a strategy for new restaurant

Dozens of restaurants cater for the residents of Battersea, London SW11. So Martin and Vanessa Lam focused their marketing strategy for the opening of Ransome's Dock Restaurant Bar on offering quality food at affordable prices. Three months before the restaurant opened, information was sent to all the media food writers. Then a simple brochure with a background to the restaurant, a sample menu, prices and map was distributed to selected households and streets within one mile of the restaurant. From the *Yellow Pages*, local businesses were also contacted, concentrating on advertising and media companies.

20.5.93

Caterer & Hotelkeeper, Sandra Lawson and Alastair Stevenson

On producing printed promotional material

conform to your house style/corporate identity

balance economy of long print runs with likelihood that the information may become out of date (e.g. reorganisation of telephone codes, change in personnel)

proof read with great care, check once for sense, check again looking at each word (a useful technique is to read the lines backwards)

take particular care with headings, captions, and details you are familiar with: the danger is that the eye and brain assume it is correct

when briefing designers, printers and suppliers of merchandise, leave nothing to chance

ask to see samples of paper, texture and colours

double check: any possibility of misunderstanding, the likelihood is that it will occur

On producing printed promotional material

On producing printed promotional material

Countdown to opening

Sedgebrook Hall, in the middle of Northamptonshire, markets itself as a purpose-built conference centre, not a hotel with bolt-on facilities. The latter, believes Norman Bellone, general manager, offers too many distractions.

The Hall is firmly closed to the general public. Cross-fertilisation would fragment the business. But there are two exceptions: a 200-strong private leisure club, and no-expense-spared weddings, marketed through a glossy brochure and magazine advertising.

Bellone primed his potential market with thousands of mailshots showing an acorn, with the message that the conference centre would open in 90 days. The next mailshot had the acorn opening to an oak: 'another 60 days to go'.

22.10.92

Caterer & Hotelkeeper, Penny Wilson

On keeping on the right side of the law

- make no misleading claims in advertisements or promotional material

- register with the Data Protection Registrar (tel: 01625 545 740) that you hold computer-based information on people (this includes mailing lists and guest history records)

- do not fax private individuals (in a direct selling campaign) without their prior consent

- consult the Fax Preference Service (tel: 0845 070 0702) to check that businesses you propose faxing (in a direct selling campaign) have not put themselves on the call-barring list

- consult the Mailing Preference Service (tel: 0345 034599) for telephone numbers and addresses of people who do not want to receive direct sales (unsolicited) material

Telesales

From your experience of taking such calls, you will be aware of the increasing use of telesales by large companies especially, and if you do not have staff to filter them for you, their potential to irritate. Phoning at a time when everyone should know a publican or hotelier is busy. Obviously reading from a script. Drawing you into a long conversation before revealing the cost. The give-away signs that it is a sales call, 'May I speak to the proprietor or manager?'

So, avoid such mistakes! Instead, follow the techniques that distinguish the successful operators:

- find out and use the name of the person you are calling

- have a reason for your call: to introduce your business, to keep contact with a regular customer, to follow up a direct mailing, to respond to an enquiry the person made, perhaps as a result of an advertisement, to get comments on a meal, stay, function, etc. which the customer has recently had

- offer benefits, e.g. a quote for a forthcoming event, special offer, room upgrade

- flatter the person you are calling, with congratulations on opening new premises, or winning a large export order

- be sensitive to indications that it is not a convenient time to talk, and arrange to call back at a suitable time

- keep records of previous contacts, interests and purchases.

Winning back the customers

Slowly but surely, Kathryn Colas persuaded customers to come back by cold calling every guest that had ever stayed at Stanhill Court in Charlwood, Surrey, telling them it was under new management. By word of mouth, the hotel was put back on the map.

28.11.96

Caterer & Hotelkeeper, Linda Fox

Discipline your thoughts. What is it you want to say? Prepare a simple script to keep you on track. Say who you are and where you're calling from. Make sure that your contact has time to talk; if not, establish a more suitable time for you to call back.

Who should you call? Here the value of your customer database comes into play. You already have a relationship with those customers and a call will usually be welcome, even if it does come as a surprise. It will remind them of your relationship and often trigger off a new booking.

I suggest you start modestly, perhaps making just 10 calls a day at first, in whatever is the quietest period for your business.

Glenmore Trenear-Harvey in *Hotel & Restaurant*

Email

You need a reasonably fast and powerful computer, a modem or ISDN line, a service provider and the software to get started. If your business has an email address, the email addresses of customers who contact you by this means can very easily be captured in your address book. Others can be added from business cards, letterheads, invoices and adverts of those you wish to target: follow the use of lower/upper case accurately, get spelling and the position of full-stops, hyphens and other punctuation correct.

The speed and ease of email, the flexibility to send photographs and longer documents as attached files, and the low cost once you are set up, give it great potential. Few people can resist looking at an email the moment it arrives, in case it is an important communication.

However, there is already a backlash against unsolicited email, especially when the message has little significance to the recipient. People are also suspicious of viruses that arrive in attached documents.

Email lunch order

Office workers who want a quick breakfast, lunch, or snack, but more than a sandwich, can email, telephone or call in at the deli at the Great Portland Street branch of the restaurant Mash, open from 8 am to 10 pm. The extensive range has recently been added to with Mashboxes. These contain a daily-changing choice of fish, meat or vegetarian lunch or dinner. Breakfast boxes are also available, to be joined shortly by luxury or speciality boxes.

A colour brochure advertising the service will be distributed to local companies as well as party organisers.

21.5.98

Caterer & Hotelkeeper, Linda Fox

On-line delivery for Indian cuisine

A new service to office workers is being launched by Iqbal Wahhab of Cinnamon Club. 'The days of long lunches in the City [of London] are long gone. Nowadays, everyone is stuck at their desks.'

Wahhab's system will operate through email to specific businesses. The office worker brings up the daily-changing menu, makes a choice and sends a return email. The first time the customer makes an order, credit card details and location in the office will be recorded. From that point, the customer is billed on a monthly basis.

At the production kitchen, orders will be automatically printed on labels by the computer. Deliveries will be made to each office at the same time every day. Recipes for chicken tikka, kebab in a roll, and various rice and curry meals have been adapted so dishes are easier to eat at a desk and won't 'stink the office out'.

19.2.98

Caterer & Hotelkeeper, Rosalind Mullen

Internet

This gives you access to anyone who uses a computer on-line to find information on where to visit, stay, eat and drink. Websites vary from words and simple graphics, to photographs, interactive maps, virtual buildings, menus, enquiry and booking facilities, and sound effects.

To have your own website, you rent storage from a service provider. You can develop your own design and content, or pay someone to do it. You can also buy into larger websites, supplying the information and perhaps photographs to their specification. These are like guidebooks, in which you pay to participate.

Information on your business – researched from guides, tourist board information, etc. and possibly from personal experience as a customer – may already appear as part of websites maintained by enthusiasts and organisations which promote the region or area.

How those using the Internet find your website or entry is crucial. A popular way is to use one of the web's search engines to find 'hotels', 'pubs', 'restaurants' in specified places, regions or countries. Alternatively, a visit to one website leads to linked sites. Successful finds may then be added to the person's directory of favourites, in order to go straight to the website another time.

Spend some time 'surfing the net' yourself, to check different ways in which enquirers can get to your site. Contact the various search engines to register your own site. Put your website address on stationery, in guide book entries and advertisements.

Good conversion rate, low cost

An 18-bedroom one-crown hotel in London gets more than 100 enquiries a month from people surfing the Internet in countries as diverse as Estonia and Zaire. A quarter of these become firm bookings. Bhupinder Bhasin, who helps his parents run the hotel, developed the website himself to keep the cost down. It works out at about £20 a month, or 50p per room let.

5.2.96

Caterer & Hotelkeeper

It's easy to be ensnared by the equivalent of the rogue hotel guide publishers. I regularly come across new companies selling web page advertising to hotels. Most have no experience or knowledge of marketing hotels, and can be merely a one-man band with a personal computer. Don't part with your money until you have credible assurances on how the website will be promoted via the Internet search engines. Otherwise, looking for a web page for a hotel in a particular area can be a lot like looking for a needle in a haystack.

You should also check how many users can access the website at any one time (you don't want the equivalent of an 'engaged' signal when they try to look at your web pages). How many 'hits' a day does that site get (this is equivalent to circulation figures)? And what does the site offer? There's no benefit in being one of a half-dozen hotels in a site full of tinkers, tailors and candlestick makers.

Graham Tayler, *Caterer & Hotelkeeper*

5 Get marketing

The time has come to make plans and get the process underway. Review and learn from experience as you do so, and measure the results. Marketing is an evolving process. Activities and events occur that you have not predicted. Be on the watch for changes in what your customers want, and new markets which offer potential if you can adjust your product. Continue to collect feedback from customers, to observe what competitors are doing, and to research local and national trends. Enjoy the success of your efforts. Be happy to welcome an increasing number of customers who return. But guard against complacency: even the best marketing cannot compensate for a product that disappoints your customers.

Evaluate each possibility

Short-list the most appropriate methods for reaching your market on the basis of:

- what has previously worked or not worked for you, and likely reasons for the success or failure

- what you have noticed competitors and similar businesses using and with what results

- how much you can afford to spend, taking into account the hoped-for results

- what resources and skills you have available to organise and carry out the activity, and the follow-up action.

Then, for each short-listed method, research in detail:

- what needs to be done, e.g. obtaining quotes from printers, booking advertising space, briefing and overseeing a designer, signing a personal letter, stuffing envelopes

- what options are available and hold most potential, e.g. series of three quarter-page advertisements in magazine A with a circulation of 20,000, or two half-pages in magazine B with a circulation of 35,000

- the costs: check against what needs to be done, so no aspect is overlooked; with brochures, ask two or three printers to quote

- the timescale involved, e.g. when space must be booked, the copy provided, publication date

- what you hope to achieve, e.g. increase weekend business by 10%, sell out the Christmas festive package.

Can't just sit back

'Everyone thinks Skye shuts down for winter', comments Jane MacLeod. From the mid-September until January, when the Atholl House hotel closes for two months, she battles to fill her 10-bedroom hotel in the north-west of the island, and to attract diners to the 40-seater restaurant.

She has started offering three-day breaks at heavily discounted rates. These are promoted on the hotel's website. To increase food and beverage revenue, she targets the local market. A steak evening proved popular. So did a murder mystery night, advertised in the local newspaper and in shop windows.

The 12-room Hotel Eilean Iarmain (open all-year-round) also steps up efforts to attract locals in the winter. Traditional music nights, and themed evenings are successful. Repeat business and word-of-mouth recommendation are relied on for filling bedrooms. Aggressive marketing to the existing database of clients is important, as Effie Kennedy explains:

'We write to people and companies and canvass all the time. You have to work at it. You can't just sit back and hope that the bookings will come in. You have to keep plugging away.'

8.1.98

Caterer & Hotelkeeper, Helen Conway

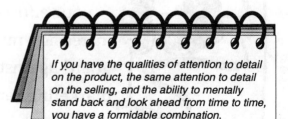

If you have the qualities of attention to detail on the product, the same attention to detail on the selling, and the ability to mentally stand back and look ahead from time to time, you have a formidable combination.

Melvyn Greene in *Hotel & Catering Business*

Checklists: establishing costs

Print

(e.g. promotional material, stationery)

- [ ] fees to any advisors, designers and consultants used to prepare copy and/or design and/or arrange supply of material
- [ ] executing illustrations, diagrams, maps, design
- [ ] search and re-use fees for any general photographs searched from a photographic library
- [ ] photographer's fees, plus travel, film, developing and printing expenses
- [ ] re-use fees
- [ ] typesetting and preparation of artwork
- [ ] proof-reading (if done professionally)
- [ ] additional charges for corrections
- [ ] printing: scanning of photographs and illustrations; typesetting and other pre-press costs in the control of the printer; paper; number and choice of colours; quantity; finishing (folding, collating, wire stitching, laminating, varnishing, etc.); delivery

Direct mail

- [ ] (if used) copy-writing
- [ ] design and production of enclosures (letter, brochure, reply card, etc. – see Print)
- [ ] envelopes
- [ ] purchasing/renting/ maintaining mailing lists
- [ ] addressing/personalising letters
- [ ] addressing envelopes/labels
- [ ] filling envelopes with enclosures
- [ ] postage/hand distribution/inclusion in mail round
- [ ] fee for reply-paid service/freephone (if used)

Internet and email

- [ ] hardware and software to develop/maintain site
- [ ] consultant to develop website (if used)
- [ ] service provider's fee
- [ ] registering website address (if you want unique, short, memorable address, as in hcima.org.uk)
- [ ] establishing links from other sites (e.g. British Tourist Authority, regional tourist board)
- [ ] taking space in other websites
- [ ] on-line costs (telephone charges to access service provider)

Corporate identity

- [ ] fees to designer, PR company or studio for developing range of treatments and producing roughs of suggested logos and name-styles
- [ ] fees for preparing final artwork
- [ ] fees for designing and preparing artwork for letterhead, business cards and other stationery
- [ ] printing of stationery with new corporate design
- [ ] printing of brochures and other sales material with new corporate design
- [ ] supply of other badged items, as required (e.g. linen, uniforms, drink mats)

Signage

- [ ] local authority planning application fee
- [ ] design and artwork
- [ ] materials to construct signs
- [ ] assembly and fitting
- [ ] lighting

Advertising

- [ ] (if used) design, artwork, illustrations, photography
- [ ] (if used) copy-writing
- [ ] fee to publishers/ newspaper/broadcaster: check from rate cards (reflects circulation, size of advert/broadcast time, use of colour)

Balance price appeal with business needs

Price-based offers are powerful draws: 'free glass of wine with dinner', 'weekend breaks only £X'. The aim is to attract lots of customers – previous ones to remind them of the quality of what you offer and, hopefully, many new ones.

Much of the skill is in timing: winning extra business when you would otherwise not be busy. And pitch: attracting customers who would not otherwise be buying at that price. To achieve a balance with business needs:

- avoid offers which jeopardise otherwise full-paying custom

- choose packages that will stimulate the sales of other, more profitable, products alongside the special offer

- state conditions – the 'small print' – concisely, and avoid ambiguity

- brief staff who will be taking bookings and payment on the conditions and their scope to deal with border-line interpretations

- monitor the knock-on effect of the special offer: on regular customers, on sales and profits of individual products, on staffing, on value of previous business generated.

Promo backfires

A chicken restaurant in London SW15 attracted the wrong publicity when shoppers using a nearby cash dispenser were alarmed to see people wearing paper bags over their heads. The police intervened to ask the restaurant's public relations company to halt the campaign.

Regular customers had been offered two meals for the price of one if they walked into the restaurant wearing one of the brown paper bags with perforated eyeholes that had been put through their letter boxes.

The Restaurant Business

Ad + special offer brings 600 per week

Money can easily be wasted on advertising, but when it works it can be highly successful. Peter and Chris Wickham advertise special offers on meals at the Ship overlooking Chichester harbour in each issue of the *Meon Valley News*. 'In a quiet month, like January, the offer is from Sunday evening to Friday lunchtime. We get about 600 customers a week from the ad alone. At busier times of the year, we may restrict the offer to Sunday evenings.'

1.8.96

Caterer & Hotelkeeper, Michael Sargent

All sales promotions need to be properly targeted and carefully monitored. There is a barrage of questions to consider. How much extra business will it bring? Does turnover more than compensate for price reductions? Are you damaging longer term prospects for a short-term boost to cash flow?

Remember, too, it is easy to give things away, but can be difficult to go back to full pricing. Price reductions or special offers should be strictly defined. Do not make open commitments.

Michael Sargent, *Caterer & Hotelkeeper*

When and how to get professional help

You know your business better than anyone, but sometimes outside advice can provide that perspective you would otherwise have missed, and save money by suggesting avenues you had not thought of.

Check the telephone directory to contact business advisory, development and training organisations in your area. Members may be able to get advice and contact details of recognised consultants through their professional body, trade association, tourist board (see page 29), or chamber of trade.

However, when you have a limited budget and modest plans, it will not normally be necessary, to employ a marketing consultant. Instead:

- by asking, you can get much useful advice from advertising departments, printers and designers – they would rather have your regular business, as a result of giving sound advice

- when editors do not use your press releases, phone and ask if there was any particular reason

- show designs for advertisements, leaflets and brochures to your staff and friends, and ask for their frank reaction.

How to get the best from a consultant

A good consultant will provide an objective third-party view and the benefit of his or her experience. Not exhausted by the daily grind of running a restaurant or hotel, consultants can bring fresh ideas, generate plenty of enthusiasm and so help you to boost business.

what do you want the consultant to do?
jot down your objectives, explain your needs fully, describe current practices and developments to give the consultant a clear understanding of your needs

what is the consultant's expertise?
ask for references and examples of past projects, speak to past clients about the consultant's work; is there after-sales service; who in a large company will work on the project?

what will it cost?
check consultant's daily rate, how many days will be required, what additional charges there might be, e.g. postage and travel, when payments will be expected, and review and agree a written contract before work starts

what format should the report take?
state how much detail you need, what kind of background information you require, and how you intend to use the report

what information already exists?
make available any relevant reports so the consultant doesn't duplicate material

what is your timescale?
ask the consultant to suggest project stages, so the work proceeds as you envisage, and time is not spent on aspects you don't wish to cover, and insist on regular update meetings

are you committed?
you learn more by being fully involved and this can reduce costs because you provide relevant information and contacts

what if you are not satisfied?
discuss your doubts as early as possible so that mistakes or misinterpretations can be rectified: don't wait for the final invoice

are you prepared to implement the findings?
using a consultant is an expensive way of postponing uncomfortable action

Make a plan

Inevitably, this takes time and you are unlikely to cover every eventuality. But the process brings a useful discipline to your thoughts, ideas and ambitions. It frees you to concentrate on the activities themselves, so you can get the best results for your money and resources.

The plan does not have to be a formal document, although you will find it helpful to have a summary, in note form if this is easier. You then have a memory prompt, a record of your reasoning, something to check back on as the results come through, and an aid for future planning.

Build in contingencies. Reflect as you make your plan, on what could go wrong, and if so how you can minimise the negative consequences. Such as:

- an overwhelming response – how to re-stock quickly, support your staff and recruit extra help, steps to keep customers informed of possible delays, and satisfactory ways of apologising for delays

- a price-based promotion attracts the wrong business – what extras you can promote to boost profits, how to reduce costs, ways to retain (and perhaps reward) the loyalty of regular customers.

Aim for a sustained effort, so that you can benefit from the cumulative effect of your marketing. Customers get regular reminders. You establish a more predictable pattern of business. The lead time for new initiatives to bring results is reduced.

Award-winning marketing campaign

As an independent hotel, the Alexander family's new venture, the 65-bedroom Castle Green hotel, could find itself relying on tourist trade to the Lake District and would, therefore, be vulnerable in winter. So locals became the target market: 'The Kendal hotel for Kendal people'.

The assault on the locals started four months before the hotel's opening. The summer garden party led to 25 Christmas bookings. There was also a barbecue, and some 200 prominent local people were invited to a dinner dance, attracting extensive press coverage and raising £2500 for local charities. The opening on December 1st was marked by a firework display. All in all, the campaign succeeded in pulling 6000 local people through the hotel.

The Alexanders made sure they had as much coverage as possible in the local media. The hotel was featured in a three-month series of advertisements in the *Westmorland Gazette*. Lord Cavendish was invited to turn the first sod, an event which was shown on local Border TV. There was also a teaser campaign of 240 ten-second slots on Bay Radio. And the Alexanders made personal visits to all businesses in Kendal.

During the building works, telephone enquiries were handled at all times of the day. And some 300 prospective customers were given a 'hard-hat tour' of the function rooms.

The targets – to achieve 6000 pre-Christmas party covers and banqueting sales of £150,000 between 3 and 23 December – were exceeded, by 15% and 20% respectively. The outlay was only £15,000.

Caterer & Hotelkeeper: Castle Green Hotel won the 1998 Cateys award for the best independent marketing campaign

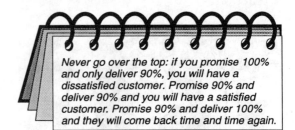

Never go over the top: if you promise 100% and only deliver 90%, you will have a dissatisfied customer. Promise 90% and deliver 90% and you will have a satisfied customer. Promise 90% and deliver 100% and they will come back time and time again.

Melvyn Greene, *Hotel & Caterer Business*

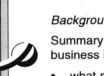

Marketing plan

Background

Summary of where your business is now:

- what makes your business special
- main products and services
- principal customer groups
- competitors
- recent developments affecting your product and your customers
- analysis of the strengths, weaknesses, opportunities and threats.

Aims

State concisely:

- target markets, e.g. previous customers, families, pensioners, office workers, single travellers
- products to be marketed, e.g. weekend breaks, quiz nights, Sunday lunches, with relevant information on timing
- business targets, e.g. to attract twice the number of women customers, to serve an average of 150 dinners per week, to increase bar revenue by 15%
- secondary objectives, e.g. to win back customers from competing businesses, to gain a reputation for excellence, to develop European market

Outline of campaign and budget

Overview of the marketing methods you will use, what each is expected to achieve, overall budget and breakdown by activity, phasing of activities.

Methods, timings and costs

List proposed activities with key details:

- corporate identity: preferred typefaces, colours and sizes, logo or design
- signage: location, purpose, planning permission requirements, design and production arrangements
- in-house selling: who will be involved, training, products to be promoted, measuring results, incentive scheme
- face-to-face or direct selling: source for contacts, who makes sales call, where, follow-up arrangements
- merchandising: advertising message/purpose, production and distribution; for in-house displays: purpose, location, how products to be displayed
- guide books: readership, editorial focus, reputation, basis for inclusion
- consortia: organisations to consider joining, benefits and costs, requirements to meet, action plan for forming local consortium
- tourist board registration: criteria to meet, cost, likely benefits, target grade to achieve, action to be taken
- public relations: involvement in local events, charities and community projects, joint activities, news stories for press releases, press and other key contacts to entertain
- advertising: titles, circulation and target audience, date for copy/artwork and who will prepare, space required, response mechanism
- direct mail: what to send, address sources, distribution
- telesales: who to call, sources for telephone numbers and names, who will make the call, what to say, logging follow-up
- email: source of addresses, attachments to be sent
- Internet: specification for website, enquiry and booking facilities, links to other sites, registering with search engines, other web sites to buy into.

Briefing staff

Involve your staff:

- what you are doing and hope to achieve, their role
- invite their comments at the planning stage: how would they and friends react as potential customers, what impact might the activity have on their work?
- how to help track responses, and get customer feedback
- how to handle enquiries
- how you want special offers dealt with for sales control purposes
- any limitations or rules governing what is available, when exceptions should be made, and how to deal with them.

Monitoring results

How you will find out and log the source of enquiries, bookings and business generated. Where possible, build in scope for modifying later stages of the campaign in the light of experience.

Keep your plan under review

Unexpected marketing opportunities are likely to arise, no matter how thorough your plan. These may come with tight deadlines and techniques to get you signed up quickly. First:

- satisfy yourself that the claims about circulation and readership are realistic: ask probing questions, review past copies of the magazine or publication, contact other advertisers to ask how satisfied they have been

- compare the cost and likely return, and that you have the budget available, just as you have done for those activities you have already planned

- how it will complement, enhance or replace other planned activities

- read the small print, be certain you are not entering a bigger commitment than it would appear.

Another aspect difficult to predict, is how the business decisions of your competitors will impact on your planned marketing activities. This may include undercutting your prices on an continuous basis, or for competing special promotions. The danger in a tit-for-tat response is that it escalates, producing the sort of price war that supermarkets and petrol stations get into from time to time. Consumers will take advantage, but generally are too canny to assume it will last, and are suspicious that other prices have been increased to compensate.

Instead, re-emphasise what makes your business special. Concentrate even more on the quality of what customers get. Make this more important to them than saving a few pounds.

Film fame, if you insist

Insisting on a credit for its use as a location during the making of *Four Weddings and a Funeral*, brought the Crown Hotel in Amersham, Bucks up to 15 calls a day from people who wanted to book the suite used by Hugh Grant and Andie MacDowell for a bedroom scene. Because of the film's shoestring budget, the Crown only received £200 a day in fees.

By comparison, the St James Court in London got £1000 per day for *Howard's End*, and the Randolph Hotel in Oxford £5000 for a three-day shoot to *Shadowlands*, which involved completely remodelling two public rooms.

The cardinal rule, warns Andrew Buchanan, Randolph's general manager, is to check out the fee, access requirements, insurance, supply of electricity, and every other detail before letting a film crew loose in your hotel – and put it in a formal contract.

20.2.97

Caterer & Hotelkeeper

Internet interest

In the three months since setting up a site with three major web sites specialising in hotels, the 11-bedroom Royal Oak of Luxborough in Exmoor National Park has had a large number of enquiries and one booking that netted £500, enough to pay the total setting up cost. Advertising and tourist guides, on which Kevan Draper spent £2500 in the previous year, failed to generate as much interest.

Furthermore, 'any enquiry via the Internet is direct, with no middleman or booking agency fees. The return response is quick and can be very informative and interactive – you can send maps, details of places of interest and menus. It is very cost-effective: no need to send brochures, envelopes or stamps. Rates and descriptions can be changed at will.'

10.9.98

Caterer & Hotelkeeper, Kevan Draper in Viewpoint

Coping with an award

Being made Restaurant of the Year by a local newspaper, changed the course of Ian Guthrie's business for good. 'Up to that time, we considered ourselves a "momma and poppa" business – a small hotel with a low-key restaurant providing good food for guests and their visitors from a limited menu.

'But the award attracted customers for whom we were not catering, and we had to decide whether to change to suit them and grow. Big decisions followed, all made in a hurry and for which we were not prepared. With our lack of experience, we nearly fell flat on our faces.'

Flattered to be selected for an award, your first thought is that it is about time all your hard work and talent was acknowledged. The second thought is about all the lovely free publicity.

But before accepting the award, it is wise to consider how you can cope with the extra business. Will it change the nature or scale of your business and, if so, is that what you want? What revision will your business plan need? What training and support will staff need? Can they be prepared in time? Is customer perception likely to change? Will greater volume affect quality?

11.7.96

Caterer & Hotelkeeper, Ian Guthrie in Viewpoint

Ensure that you have made and are making 'reasonable adjustments' to provide for disabled people, such as disability equality training for staff who have customer/guest contact, offering to read menus and describe position of food on plate to anyone with sight difficulties.

Since 1 October 1999, under the phased introduction of the provisions of the Disability Discrimination Act 1995, it has been unlawful for service providers to discriminate against disabled people. From 2004, you will also have to make 'reasonable adjustments' to your premises to overcome physical barriers to access.

Decision and vigilance pays

It is three years since Nicholas Malcolm decided not to mix clients. Since then children have ruled the roost at Travelgue hotel in Torquay. Malcolm advises adults without children to stay elsewhere.

But with so many children, the toys and equipment provided by the hotel take a fair bashing and need to be updated regularly. With 60% of Travelgue business repeat custom, Malcolm recognises the continual need for innovation: 'Children are so prone to boredom.'

And supervised creche facilities, undoubtedly a key attraction for parents, so they can enjoy a few hours to themselves, can involve expensive arrangements with the local authority.

31.3.94

Caterer & Hotelkeeper, Jenny Webster

Measure results

Marketing should make a positive impact on turnover and profitability, but a whole range of factors can affect sales and costs such as:

- sales: changes in spending patterns of customers reflecting national and local socio-economic trends, competitors' activities, weather, popularity and number of events/attractions which draw people to your area, major sporting and other spectator events, marketing by the tourist boards, transport developments

- costs: staffing, food and drink purchases, cleaning materials, rates, insurance, breakages, linen and equipment replacement.

To help distinguish from such factors, the results of specific types of marketing, use the information you collect on your business pattern and your customers (Section 1). For example an increase in:

- functions and other special events, following a direct sales campaign to local businesses and organisations

- lunch time customers, following a two-for-one or other price-based promotion targeted at shoppers, by distributing leaflets to passers-by, advertising in free local newspapers and display panels on the pavement

- sales of dishes of the day/particular drinks, following the use of tent cards on tables, menu blackboards and direct selling by staff.

The link is less easy to establish for more general marketing activities, such as a new brochure, advertising in a guide, mailing Christmas cards to customers.

Young help to beat competition

Unable to compete with national hotel groups offering weekend family breaks at 'silly prices', yet with the weekends quiet and weekdays likely to get that way with the conference lull period of July and August approaching, the Graves family, who own Armathwaite Hall near Keswick, Cumbria, decided to create a point of difference from competitors. Carolyn Graves and her brother Charles decided to turn to the family market to plug the gap.

The first job was a new pricing structure: for up to two children under 12, sharing their parents' room on a minimum two-night half-board break, accommodation, breakfast and a standard high tea would be free. 'You may get a few children who eat a big breakfast, but at the end of the day, a child costs very little,' maintains Carolyn.

To provide the something extra, the Graves hit upon a junior activity programme, to keep children occupied and give parents a few hours off. With the exception of a small supplement for the gourmet dinner and the barbecue high tea, the programme is free.

To check the project was on the right lines, an advert was placed in local papers for 'young hotel inspectors'. From 100 applicants who gave their reasons why they would make good hotel inspectors, six were invited with their families to stay free of charge. As well as rating individual activities while at Armathwaite, the young inspectors had to write a follow-up report.

Chocolate cooking, the junior gourmet dinner and survival training – including how to light a fire and which plants are safe to eat – were the most popular activities. And because of its unusual nature, local press picked up the story, providing valuable publicity.

Family business is up 25% since targeting began, and annual turnover by 6%.

24.8.95

Caterer & Hotelkeeper, Jenny Webster

Market your business

On theme evenings:

◆ choose your cuisine carefully, no point in offering blinis and caviar when much of your business base is the beer and skittle type

◆ involve your staff, otherwise people will think it's a bore and a bind

◆ the details count, it's what distinguishes your theme evenings from competitors.

Making yourself focus

Offering a good product, coupled with shrewd marketing and promotion, have taken annual sales at the Brickmakers Arms in Windlesham, Surrey from £96,600 to over £825,000 in eight years. Gerry Price now employs 14 full-time staff including six chefs, and 21 part-timers.

At the beginning of each year, Price sets aside 2% of his expected turnover for the marketing and promotions programme. Every week, he analyses turnover, profit and stock levels 'so that any upward or downward trend can be spotted and acted upon immediately. It gives me a weekly view within a long-term plan. I make full use of spreadsheets: to be computer literate in this business is important.'

Promotions run for three or four months at a time, with a month-long break in between. 'This gives potential customers time to react and allows us better measurement of the promotion's effectiveness,' explains Price.

Following a mailshot to 1000 names on the customer database Price has built up, 350 people joined the Brickmakers Arms Dining Club. Members receive a 10% discount on food, except on Friday and Saturday nights. A members' dinner is held every second month and special wine prices offered. Those living within a particular radius of the restaurant can be picked up before dinner and dropped off afterwards by the Brickmakers' minibus.

Twice a year, Price holds a golfing day for 36 regular customers. They play nine holes at a nearby golf course, return to the restaurant for breakfast, play their second nine and return for

lunch. The cash returns are not vast, but 'binding diners and drinkers is always a good thing – there are people who visit again, and everyone, including my staff, enjoy the day.'

Price has also been running a two-for-one dining offer. A mailing to directors, managers and business owners in the region didn't work as well as hoped, so the leaflet was mailed again, this time to their personal assistants 'with much greater success. This promotion pays for itself. There are the wine and bar sales and often four or more people come in at a time. It's an excellent way of creating new regular customers.' Out of 930 mailings, Price had 50 returns in the first three months.

Another promotion offers £5 off any bottle of wine. Using the Royal Mail, Price sends about 10,000 flyers a month to all ABC1 households in a seven-mile radius. Colour-coding helps determine which areas are responding best. The average cost of 15p per flyer, including paper, printing, delivery and Price's time, 'is not bad really. During these promotions, there are a great deal of new faces in the restaurant. We also prime the staff to deal with any new customers, those who may not be familiar with the Brickmakers Arms.'

Asked to sum up the secret of his success, Price says: 'Results may be factual, anecdotal or emotional, but putting them down on paper is a great way of making yourself focus on what is and isn't working.'

2.97

Hotel & Catering Business, Ben Whitworth

Get feedback

A second group of measures can usefully capture trends and reactions to specific activities. You can:

- give box numbers or departments, or ask for a reference to be quoted, in response to advertisements

- give a made-up name (e.g. Lucy or Jack) as the personal contact: do brief everyone answering the phone or dealing with the post

- ask when a booking is made, how the customer heard of your business

- include such a question on comment cards or questionnaires – preferably so that people only have to tick boxes

- use distinct colours, designs or a numbering system on coupons and vouchers that customers use to claim a special offer, or get more information

- only use one activity to promote a particular special offer, e.g. posters in local newsagents advertising pensioners' lunch special

- log responses to telesales and direct sales, and track subsequent business

- keep individual records of sales made by serving staff (fairly straightforward with suitable tills or computerised ordering technology)

- employ a press cuttings agency to monitor media coverage and supply cuttings. If you are using a public relations consultant, this service may be part of the package, as it gives the consultant a means of demonstrating effectiveness to clients.

With thousands of the visitors expected for London Restaurant Week, Islington restaurateurs collaborated to organise street parties and a 'Dinner for a Tenner' promotion. Average takings increased by 20%.

A mailshot to existing customers to tell them that the Fauconberg Arms in Yorkshire was taking part in The Times 'Lunch for £5' promotion, brought 1600 visits to Robin and Nicky Jaques' restaurant.

A website established for only £480 by Mike Elvis, generated at least 500 bookings during 1998, for his Woodfalls Inn in the New Forest. Some were from as far afield as the West Coast of the United States, Canada and Peru.

Sales of each menu item are continually monitored by chef David Massey at the Brompton Bay in London. This helps ensure that the demands of customers are always met.

Using peer pressure

Concerned about a drop in beverage sales, Olivier Delaunoy, front of house general manager at Le Petit Blanc in Oxford, decided to produce individual performance reports: something in a simple format that could be given out at weekly staff meetings. All staff could then see how they had done, and equally importantly, how their colleagues had done.

A simple formula is used to work out the week's performance league table. A bottle of champagne goes to the person with the highest score, while the monthly winner gets a £25 gift voucher.

Results have been impressive, with beverage sales up from 35% to 39% of total spend, some staff occasionally breaking the 50% barrier.

1.5.97

Caterer & Hotelkeeper, Jane Cartwright

Get the best value

After enjoying the satisfaction of getting a good response to your marketing, take a harder look at the costs and benefits of each activity. On the cost side, consider:

- the involvement required of you and your staff

- direct costs incurred, e.g. designing, printing and distributing a leaflet

- any adverse impact on other customers or sources of business, e.g. having to turn away people prepared to pay the full price.

Benefits might include:

- increase in sales of the product, with improved gross profit, additional spending on related products and those on which gross profit is higher

- more customers, and new customers who return

- additional goodwill, raised profile in the marketplace

- busier atmosphere which customers and staff like

- keeping valued staff, who otherwise could not be afforded or become demotivated and move elsewhere

- contribution to fixed costs: any income is better than none (provided it is not a loss) when you have to pay electricity, rent, rates, loan interest, telephone, staff wages and other costs.

Such an analysis, even if there is only time to do it at a rather general level, will aid future decisions. It makes you look at the overall situation, knock-on costs and benefits.

Tactics change after poor response to ad

Following the strategy which had been successful for the launch of their Storyteller restaurant in Norway, Lavelle and Larsen spent £6000 advertising in the Cheltenham local paper. After little response, the couple decided to focus on direct mail. 'It is more difficult [in the UK], so the customers you have got must stay happy. You capture the details of happy customers and then send them information about ongoing activities in the restaurant.'

Two databases have been developed. For the first, individuals who had visited during the summer were called and asked if they would like to receive the restaurant's newsletter. And the bills were redesigned, to encourage customers to leave their names and addresses. Around 50 new customers are added to the database each week.

For the second database, a part-timer was engaged to work on a list of 1000 businesses with more than 10 employees in and around Cheltenham. This list has been honed down, to about a third this length, to whom Christmas menus have been sent.

Public relations is also key to the marketing strategy. A consultant has been hired to write press releases and newsletters, and organise media events to project the image of the restaurant. 'That image is adventurous. We have adventurous food and wine and we are adventurous because we fly balloons [the couple launched a hot air balloon from the North Pole in 1989]. We will have guest chefs and we will adopt a vineyard. It is not a starched, boring, ordinary restaurant.'

In September, Cheltenham's mayor joined Lavelle and Larsen in re-creating a historic balloon flight from Montpellier Gardens in the centre of the town. Four newspapers carried the story, Central Television did a five minute slot, and *Cotswold Life* magazine carried a full-page colour feature. Customers have been claiming they were told to visit the restaurant by the mayor.

27.11.97

Caterer & Hotelkeeper, Sara Guild

Learn from experience

Before deciding not to repeat a marketing activity which brought just one or two responses, and insufficient income to even pay the direct costs, check whether there were other reasons for the failure such as:

- matters over which you had (or should have had) control: poor timing, unattractive design, wording which did not appeal, wrong magazine, lacked interest, clashed with major event (e.g. popular team gets through to finals of a sporting competition)

- events or other matters which could not have been predicted, e.g. major roadworks, severe weather, security incident.

Keep a record or file of your marketing activities, so that you can look back at any time to find out who was involved, what was planned, the costs, any problems encountered or mistakes made, and the benefits. Into the same file could go copies of correspondence, estimates, proofs, a copy of the final bill, the finished brochure or published advertisement.

Depending on how much you are doing, open separate files for brochures, public relations, advertising, etc. and perhaps a new file for each year.

Some winning promotions

this week
August 1999

caterer

A classic car show in the gardens of the Priory Hotel in Louth, Lincolnshire brought people and their cars from as far afield as Frankfurt. Besides introducing hundreds of potential customers, Proprietor Colin Hillyard said the event proved great fun for his staff.

Every Monday to Friday lunchtime an average of 60 sausage meals are served at The Hope, a smallish pub in London's Tottenham Street. Roger Fonseca has built his trade in under four years, using leaflets and blackboards to promote the sausage theme.

Couples trying for a millennium baby over the weekend of 27–28 March 1999 could enjoy a four poster bed, spa bath, oysters and champagne at The Pear Tree Hotel, Purton near Swindon. If a baby duly appears on 1 January 2000 the new family gets a free weekend break in 2000 and £100 worth of Mother Care vouchers, owner Francis

Bird watching weekends along the Norfolk coast, accompanied by a local ornithologist, are bringing new business to Congham Hall.

Bonnybridge is famed for its UFO sitings. Paul Colquhoun of the Comfort Inn in nearby Falkirk has capitalised on this by offering a UFO themed weekend. Friday nights' programmes include documentaries and sci-fi shows, and on Saturdays there is a tour of UFO landing sites.

Free lunches for life are available at a restaurant in San Francisco if you agree to be tattooed with its logo. So far 41 people have done so.

Free tea or coffee if you order a specific dessert has boosted sales of desserts for Lincoln-based Jay-Dees family restaurants. 'It seems that you don't necessarily have to give much away, but you do have to continually run some sort of promotion,' commented John Downs.

To bring in corporate trade for lunch at 153 Restaurant & Bar, in Coventry's Hylands Hotel, Barbara Swan initiated 'Business Express'. She faxed the menu to 34 solicitors, 27 estate agents, 7 surveyors and 11 employment agencies, all within 10 minutes' walking distance of 153. Busy professionals tick their order and fax it back an hour before they arrive.

6 Build for the future

In the hospitality business, your customers' expectations are influenced by fashion, the media (especially television), what technology has made available in and outside the home and at workplaces, and their own experience – especially of standards and value for money which they get on holidays outside the UK. You are compared to the best, rarely the worst (would you want to be?). To avoid disappointing, you must keep your business in line with what the customers of today expect, and, importantly, those of tomorrow and beyond that. There are also legal requirements to keep step with. While there remains scope for good 'old fashioned' standards, this must be in the wider context of providing comfort and convenience.

Exploit new opportunities

You can react to change, for example customers asking for a drink which has become fashionable. You can anticipate change, for example that a road improvement scheme will bring more day trippers to the area. You can be in the forefront of change, for example with digital televisions and use of the Internet.

At one level, it is a matter of protecting your existing business: not losing out because customers expect something better or different, or are attracted elsewhere. At another level, it is a way of maintaining your appeal, showing customers that you care for them and don't take their business for granted.

Then there are the occasional chance events which turn into real money-spinners. A TV programme or film which includes scenes made in your locality, or, better still, your building. An archaeological discovery nearby which captures the public imagination. A visit from, or an incident involving, a well-known person which gets national media coverage.

Success leads to joint initiative

A traditional age-old inn is how Paul Whittome describes the Hoste Arms in Burnham Market. 'Equal importance is placed on the provision of accommodation, food and drink for locals as well as travellers.'

The success of his formula led Paul to join forces with Sir Thomas Ingilby, proprietor of the Boars Head in Ripley, establish a marketing consortium. Another 9 small inns have joined them. Membership is by invitation only.

1.10.98

Caterer & Hotelkeeper

Survey points way to pleasing women

Many bars and hotels are sexist. A typical complaint is that male room service staff tend to leer when delivering breakfast to a female guest.

Of the lone women travellers, MPs and business executives, questioned by researchers for the 5-star Athenaeum Hotel in London:

- 70% felt they had received secondary service because of their gender
- 74% said that when dining with a man, waiters assumed that the man was choosing the wine and settling the bill
- 41% felt uncomfortable when dining alone
- 62% prefer to eat in their bedroom.

The survey found that the average woman business traveller is particular about the location and business facilities of the hotel. Details that escape the notice of most men are important, such as late night ironing services, warning about any local areas considered unsafe for women, and where to get your hair done.

10.9.98

Caterer & Hotelkeeper, Christina Golding

Buy your take-away here

Noting the custom of buying food on the way home from the pub, Rose Cunningham, licensee of the Old Crown in Fleckney, Leicestershire decided there was no reason why she should not meet this demand herself. Her customers can now leave with a curry take-away.

13.5.99

Caterer & Hotelkeeper

Network, enquire, observe

Be open to ideas and suggestions. Networking with fellow businesses is invaluable: by attending trade exhibitions, through membership of industry as well as local associations. So are the Internet, industry journals, travel and consumer features and reports in the media.

Check out your local papers. Scan the announcements of engagements, birthdays and funerals. Also the advertisements to do with licensing, planning applications and changes to roads and public rights of way.

Talk to customers and sales representatives whose interests might be relevant. You can get early news on businesses setting up, a change in timing or routing of a car rally, and extra development funding.

When buying new equipment, software or systems, exploit its potential to add to the information you collect on business patterns (pages 14 and 48).

When you travel further afield, assess what other pubs, restaurants, hotels, etc. offer and how they are run. Copy or adapt ideas you like. With a disappointing experience, ask whether that might happen to your customers, and if so what extra training or investment is required.

Keep an eye on the wider issues such as economic, political and social changes, new legislation and government policies which will impact on your key markets, and how you operate your business.

Winning formula adjusted

The educated, well travelled and cosmopolitan crowd of the famous university town of Cambridge is catered for at 22 Chesterton Road, a fine dining restaurant. Achieving an average spend of between £30 and £35 per head, and gross profit rarely below 70%, encouraged David Carter and Louise Compton to branch out.

But to get an affordable lease, they had to settle on Newmarket. It was clear that the 22 Chesterton Road concept would not translate well to a less sophisticated core of local customers. So a more relaxed atmosphere has been created in Brasserie 22. An average spend of £16 to £20 per person has been achieved, but it is possible to turn tables, so the throughput can reach up to 60 covers at weekends.

1.10.98

Caterer & Hotelkeeper

CD-Rom marketing opportunity

The Western Appleby Manor, a 30-bedroom hotel, produced 3000 CD-Roms to mail to the corporate market and give to guests. The costs were underwritten by the Department of Trade and Industry, as part of a project to publicise multimedia in business. Although the Appelby Manor CD-Rom was quite expensive, involving professionals, off-the-shelf CD-Rom presentation packages for PCs are reasonably priced.

Nick Sinscoe, managing partner, has found that 'potential guests who have seen a CD-Rom are twice as likely to book at the hotel than those receiving just a traditional brochure.'

Sales staff of the Intercontinental chain, use CD-Roms to do a full colour presentation on the hotel from their laptops, and as photo libraries, so that clients can see conference and meeting rooms in various settings. These pictures can be sent as email attachments.

It is easy to keep CD-Roms up-to-date, says Richard Hyde, marketing development manager at Intercontinental. One way is to program the CD-Rom to automatically retrieve the latest information, such as a price list, from a website.

25.6.98

Caterer & Hotelkeeper, Lee Kimber

Revisit your business analysis

Marketing is one facet of running a successful business. Somehow, you have to keep the various strands together, so that the balance is achieved between:

- regular customers: pleasing them, obtaining their feedback, appreciating their loyalty

- attracting new customers: to extend your customer base, to become the regular customers of the future

- products and services: offering what satisfies customers, monitoring quality, responding to complaints, meeting requirements of tourist boards, consortia and guide books

- marketing activities employed: to be cost-effective, to maintain a presence in the marketplace, to react to changing competition and circumstances, to promote new products and services

- pricing: providing value for money, keeping your position in the market, achieving a return on your time and financial investment, generating funds for re-investment

- staffing: to deliver quality products and service, to cope with varying levels of business, to provide motivation, to develop a strong team, to improve skills and productivity, to retain valued team members

- quality of life: to reward your efforts, to provide for the future.

Nothing stands still for long in business (or life). Reviewing your business, planning and marketing, assessing the results, monitoring competition and trends, re-assessing the future – these need to be a circular, on-going process.

Benefits from catching the public mood

Gaining an Organic Restaurant Certificate, awarded by the Soil Association, has boosted turnover for Penrhos Court Hotel and Restaurant at Kington, Herefordshire by 40%. Obviously welcome news for proprietors Martin Griffiths and Daphne Lambert. 'We've been organic since we started the restaurant 25 years ago, but we've never said much about it.' All the restaurant's suppliers are registered with the Soil Association (a condition for the award). Home grown produce must also conform to the Association's principles.

Spokesman for the Association explained that the certificate is a 'relatively new venture, but the public are demanding organic food and we're delighted to help.'

19.11.98

Caterer & Hotelkeeper, Jane Baker

Labelling reassures

The BSE crisis hit sales of beef dishes throughout the industry. But not for long at Nicole's in London's Bond Street. Home-made beef burgers, rib eye steaks, chunky roast fillet sandwiches and braised shin dishes sell as fast as Annie Wayte, executive head chef, can make them.

Prominent labelling on the menu, and well-briefed serving staff, are the clues to this success. All the beef sold at Nicole's is Glenbervie Aberdeen Angus. Not only does this provide valuable reassurance on health grounds, but recognises the more discerning approach many customers are taking to produce quality.

19.11.98

Caterer & Hotelkeeper

Imagine you're the new owner of your business. You'll be taking over in about a month. Sit down and list the changes you would make to improve results. It's best to do this when you have been on holiday, or away for a day or two.

Produce simple league tables of competitors' prices and your own for similar menus, wines and spirits, and various sources of business, such as a one-day conference, an overnight stay and weekend breaks.

Review your menus. Are they right for the different meal periods and times of the week, when the markets are different?

Think about a whole range of factors unconnected with food, such as lighting, staff training, how long customers have to wait for the bill, napkins, staff uniforms, in-house selling. Think of all the different things which can make a stay in a hotel, or a meal, a memorable experience.

Melvyn Green, *Hotel & Catering Business*

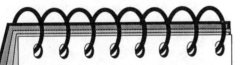

Marketing plays a fundamental role in today's business, not only in existing operations, but in shaping future developments. 'It's more complex than having large bath towels or bigger bars of soap or whatever.' Recently, two guests were overheard in the elevator, praising the standard of the hotel and the quality of the food. But one commented that he would never stay there again – because there was nowhere to plug in a laptop computer.

Thinking ahead is what marketing is about.

Adrian Simpson, interviewed by Susanna Stringer for *Caterer & Hotelkeeper's* In Focus column

Example of business co-operation

Some hotels discourage anyone who is not a guest from entering the premises. Not so the Cumberland Hotel in one of London's busiest locations, Marble Arch. Around 1600 people move in and out of the lobby daily. Paul Schnepper, general manager, has tapped into this market by:

- opening a café bar which also sells snacks in partnership with coffee company Kenco
- selling theatre tickets from a dedicated, computer-linked booth First Call
- creating a mini-business centre with fax, modem and pay telephones, in conjunction with BT – 'if people have a desk and seat, they use the telephone longer, therefore our commission increases'.

As Schnepper explains, 'Why should I mind people coming in to make a telephone call? This is a public place. For every person who walks through the lobby of the Cumberland, stops and spends 25p on a phone call, then has a cup of coffee, progresses to the Chinese restaurant and ends up having a drink in Callaghan's bar, I can be as much as £100 better off.'

16.7.98

Caterer & Hotelkeeper, Helen Conway

Match investment to your future market

Use this review and planning process to prioritise improvements to facilities, products and services:

- what will benefit existing customers and attract new customers

- what will distinguish you from, and put you ahead of the competition

- what will achieve higher grades from tourists boards and guides, and is this desirable

- what will qualify you to join marketing consortia, and is this desirable

- what will help you raise prices (if desirable), reduce operating costs, improve productivity, and handle increased trade

- what are the implications for staffing and skill requirements

- what will improve cash flow, sales and profits, reduce seasonality, make better use of facilities

- what will provide better management and marketing information

- what will qualify for financial assistance/grants/loans

- what will reduce tax liability

- what is required by government policy and legislation

- what will add to the value of the business

- what are the implications for your quality of life, and the satisfaction you get from what you are doing?

Changing direction

Two years ago, a customer split of 50% domestic and overseas tourists, 40% corporate and 10% functions was predicted in Anthony and Peta Lloyd's business plan for Fallowfields Country House Hotel and Restaurant. Today, the Lloyds earn most of their revenue from corporate business – meetings, conferences and dinners – and functions, especially weddings.

In the light of this change, what should have been good news – the granting of a licence to hold civil weddings at the hotel – presents the Lloyds with a quandary. 'Weddings tend to be booked further in advance, but the corporates are pretty inflexible and more lucrative, because they offer possibilities for repeat business.'

Anthony Lloyd hopes that careful timing will prove the answer. As not many businesses book Fridays or Mondays, he hopes to steer the weddings towards these days. This year's marketing budget of £12,000 (up 50% from the previous year) includes £1000 to advertise the hotel's marriage facilities in an Oxford registry office. Another £2200 will be spent on *Yellow Pages* advertising. Last year, an ad in the Oxford directory produced six wedding bookings. This year, the Reading and Swindon directories will also carry box adverts.

An unexpected spin-off of the ads are one-night stays and first night honeymoon bookings. 'These are all convertible', says Anthony. 'One night's dinner for two can turn into a party for 14 in a few months' time.'

The most successful direct marketing scheme last year was when Anthony mailed, then called, the top secretaries of local businesses to invite them to see the new bedrooms and conference facilities, and have lunch. He had 78 responses from a flyer sent to 400 companies, at a minimal cost. This year, there will have to be more of a 'hook' to get people back, such as a speaker, which will increase the outlay.

Anthony also plans to visit nearby business parks and companies, offering information packs to those that have never used Fallowfields. He will gather names and numbers for his database, and follow up mail-drops with telephone calls.

29/1/99

Caterer & Hotelkeeper, Beth Porter

Summary *Market your business* checklist

Take stock

- [ ] collect customer views
- [ ] track sales and take-up of products/services
- [ ] research customer base, motivation and satisfaction levels
- [ ] monitor trends in demand and expectations
- [ ] observe activities of competition

Get marketing

- [ ] check out previous results
- [ ] work within available funds, resources and skills
- [ ] timetable action to meet deadlines and produce timely results
- [ ] when using consultants, check record, brief well and agree remit
- [ ] set out your plans as a reference point and memory aide
- [ ] keep plan under review, adjust to new opportunities and events
- [ ] plan for contingencies, prepare to deal with the unexpected
- [ ] build in measures for promotional activities
- [ ] compare expectations with results
- [ ] assess impact on sales, costs, profits and customer satisfaction
- [ ] benefit from experience

Identify opportunities

- [ ] build on strengths, successes, what is popular
- [ ] acknowledge and reduce impact of weaknesses
- [ ] learn from successes and setbacks of competitors
- [ ] observe local business and community developments
- [ ] network with similar business operators
- [ ] keep track of national trends

Target extra business

- [ ] identify periods to target extra business
- [ ] value and encourage your regulars
- [ ] earn repeat custom and recommendation
- [ ] build a reputation locally
- [ ] quality control product
- [ ] act quickly to deal with complaints and disappointments
- [ ] prepare, involve and motivate staff
- [ ] focus on who and when to target
- [ ] decide what will attract
- [ ] set yourself apart from competing attractions

Review options

- [ ] develop consistent presentation of logo, business name, etc.
- [ ] attract and direct customers with effective signage
- [ ] optimise each contact with customers to sell
- [ ] use display, good presentation and merchandising to sell
- [ ] check out requests for pre-paid guide entries
- [ ] collaborate with similar businesses for stronger market presence
- [ ] join tourist board scheme for recognition and support
- [ ] build good public profile
- [ ] exploit news opportunities
- [ ] use advertisements to create interest and stimulate action
- [ ] target accurately and avoid the waste bin with direct mail
- [ ] establish person-to-person contact with planned telesales
- [ ] email for speed and convenience, respond as rapidly
- [ ] exploit the vast information resource which is the world-wide web

Index